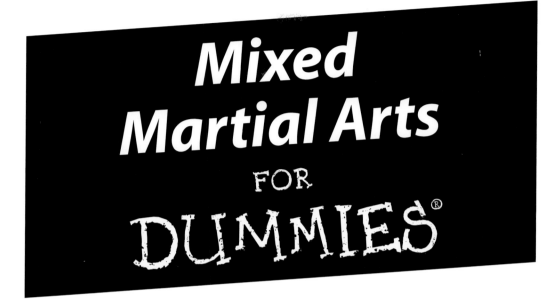

Mixed Martial Arts FOR DUMMIES®

by Frank Shamrock

with Mary Van Note

WILEY

Wiley Publishing, Inc.

Mixed Martial Arts For Dummies®

Published by
Wiley Publishing, Inc.
111 River St.
Hoboken, NJ 07030-5774
www.wiley.com

Copyright © 2009 by Wiley Publishing, Inc., Indianapolis, Indiana

Published by Wiley Publishing, Inc., Indianapolis, Indiana

Published simultaneously in Canada

For general information on our other products and services, please contact our Customer Care Department within the U.S. at 877-762-2974, outside the U.S. at 317-572-3993, or fax 317-572-4002.

For technical support, please visit www.wiley.com/techsupport.

Wiley also publishes its books in a variety of electronic formats. Some content that appears in print may not be avail-able in electronic books.

Library of Congress Control Number: 2009922967

ISBN: 978-0-470-39071-9

Manufactured in the United States of America

10 9 8 7 6 5 4 3 2 1

WILEY

About the Author

Frank Shamrock is an American mixed martial arts legend, entrepreneur, actor, nationally recognized commentator, mentor, coach, and author. Frank, who was a ward of the state of California by 11 years old, rose to become a world champion by age 22.

Also known as "The Legend," Frank Shamrock is a decorated American mixed martial arts fighter who was undefeated in combat for nearly a decade. Frank set two world records for the fastest victories in the sport and is recognized worldwide as one of the pioneers of mixed martial arts. Frank was the first fighter to hold the title of UFC middleweight champion. After defending his middleweight title five times, he retired from the UFC undefeated. Frank was crowned "King of Pancrase" at the age of 24 and was awarded the title "The Fighter of the Decade." He has also held titles as World Extreme Cagefighting light-heavyweight champion and Strikeforce middleweight champion.

Internationally known as one of the world's top martial arts instructors and trainers, Frank is a 7th Dan in Submission Fighting and the highest ranking instructor of the style in the United States. Frank runs a franchise of MMA training facilities and coaches his own fight team, "Team Shamrock." He also runs Frank Shamrock Inc., MMA Entertainment, Mixed Martial Arts for Law Enforcement, and a merchandising company.

Frank was instrumental in making mixed martial arts a respected and sanctioned sport in the United States, and he continues to promote MMA in the mainstream media. He has been seen by millions on CBC, NBC, Showtime, and pay-per-view.

Frank shares his story and journey by giving keynote speeches, offering motivational seminars, and doing charity work for underprivileged youth and juvenile detention centers. His rise to fame and commitment to the sport of MMA has inspired and encouraged people around the world to fight for a better life for themselves.

Author's Acknowledgments

I would like to acknowledge my boxing coach, Tony Demaria, for his service and guidance (and for teaching me to punch).

Carole, my literary agent, for seeing my dreams with her eyes and having the wisdom and patience to make them happen.

And finally, Mary Van Note, without whose comedy, caring, and art with words, this book would've never happened.

Dedication

I would like to dedicate this book to my wife, Amy, and two children, son Frank and baby daughter Nicolette, for teaching me about the art of living and for making that life so amazing and worthwhile.

Publisher's Acknowledgments

We're proud of this book; please send us your comments through our Dummies online registration form located at www.dummies.com/register/.

Some of the people who helped bring this book to market include the following:

Acquisitions, Editorial, and Media Development

Senior Project Editor: Tim Gallan

Acquisitions Editor: Mike Baker

Copy Editor: Jennifer Tebbe

Photographer: Jomar Enciso

Editorial Manager: Michelle Hacker

Editorial Assistants: Joe Niesen, Jennette ElNaggar, David Lutton

Cartoons: Rich Tennant (www.the5thwave.com)

Composition Services

Project Coordinators: Katie Key, Erin Smith

Layout and Graphics: Laura Campbell, Reuben W. Davis, Carrie A. Cesavice, Brent Savage, Christine Williams, Erin Zeltner

Proofreaders: John Greenough, Penny L. Stuart

Indexer: Dakota Indexing

Publishing and Editorial for Consumer Dummies

Diane Graves Steele, Vice President and Publisher, Consumer Dummies

Joyce Pepple, Acquisitions Director, Consumer Dummies

Kristin Ferguson-Wagstaffe, Product Development Director, Consumer Dummies

Ensley Eikenburg, Associate Publisher, Travel

Kelly Regan, Editorial Director, Travel

Publishing for Technology Dummies

Andy Cummings, Vice President and Publisher, Dummies Technology/General User

Composition Services

Gerry Fahey, Vice President of Production Services

Debbie Stailey, Director of Composition Services

Contents at a Glance

Table of Contents

Introduction

• •

Congratulations on taking the first step toward your new life in mixed martial arts! Also known as MMA, mixed martial arts isn't just a sport — it's also a way of life that can change you for the better physically, mentally, and spiritually.

I've been a mixed martial artist for more than 15 years and have seen the sport grow and flourish. MMA is now hugely popular in the United States and around the world, resulting in more and more young athletes wanting to get involved in the sport. Of course, this popularity has also led to a lot of people training in MMA in all the wrong ways and for all the wrong reasons. That's why I decided to write a book to teach people the virtues, ethics, and techniques of MMA, while at the same time promoting safety during training. Basically, I love MMA and want to share my love of the sport with you. Consequently, this book introduces you to the basics of MMA and eases you into your new life as a mixed martial artist.

About This Book

I believe that a good mixed martial artist is someone who's trained in multiple fighting styles. That's why this book covers both stand-up fighting and submission fighting. But MMA is about more than just punches, kicks, and takedowns. It's also about training, both mentally and physically, so much of this book focuses on helping you develop a safe and effective training regimen.

The great thing about this book is that you don't have to read it cover to cover, unless of course you want to, because I break down the concepts of MMA into parts like Stand Up and Grappling. If you're new to MMA, you may want to start with Chapter 1 so you can get an overview of the sport. If you're already training in MMA, take a look at Chapter 13 for some fight-specific training drills. Ultimately, you should feel free to skip around to whatever interests you.

Conventions Used in This Book

Mixed Martial Arts For Dummies presents step-by-step instructions on how to perform all sorts of MMA maneuvers, from strikes and holds to takedowns and escapes. But the instructions by themselves aren't all that helpful without pictures, which is why I provide multiple photos for the steps in each section. When necessary, I show multiple photos of the same step from different angles so you get a more complete picture of what's going on.

Also, sometimes certain words in a chapter appear in italics, *like this*. The italics indicate a special word or phrase that's relevant to the MMA world but that you may not be familiar with. The definition typically follows the italicized word or phrase.

Foolish Assumptions

Prepare to be shocked and amazed, but my number one foolish assumption about you is that you have an interest in MMA. Whether you're already training, want to start training, or just enjoy watching MMA bouts on television, I'm assuming that you're not only a big fan of MMA but that you also want to participate.

Because MMA is a lifestyle choice, and because a well-rounded fighter is adept in nutrition, flexibility, and strength and conditioning, I'm also assuming that you have either knowledge of or interest in some basic nutritional and exercise-related information. Granted, I spend most of my time here focusing on MMA, but I also touch on some of the aforementioned topics that help make you a well-rounded fighter. I suggest picking up some other *For Dummies* titles if you don't already have a background in nutrition and multiple exercise disciplines. Check out these titles, all of which are published by Wiley:

- *Nutrition For Dummies,* 4th Edition by Carol Ann Rinzler
- *Weight Training For Dummies,* 3rd Edition by Liz Neporent, Suzanne Schlosberg, and Shirley J. Archer
- *Exercise Balls For Dummies* by LaReine Chabut
- *Meditation For Dummies,* 2nd Edition by Stephan Bodian
- *Yoga For Dummies* by Georg Feuerstein and Larry Payne

How This Book Is Organized

In addition to ensuring this book has all the info you need to get started with your MMA training, I've also made certain that *Mixed Marital Arts For Dummies* is as easy to navigate as possible so you can get in and get out when and where you need to. The remaining pages of this book are organized into 16 chapters that are divided into five parts. Following is a brief breakdown of each part.

Part 1: Welcome to My World (Of Pain)

In this part, I take you into the world of mixed martial arts. Chapter 1 helps you explore the history of MMA and introduces you to the basics of MMA as a particular way of life. Chapter 2 presents the fighting styles that have become synonymous with modern MMA and clues you in to the rules of the game. Finally, Chapter 3 gives you the tools you need to jump-start your training.

Part II: Stand-Up Fighting

Here's everything you need to know about the position in which every MMA bout starts — the standing position. I show you essential strikes, ways to defend yourself against strikes, inside fighting with the clinch, and takedowns.

Part III: Grappling: You Gotta Have a Ground Game

In this part, I guide you in the essentials of ground fighting. You get to know the guard position (in which you're grappling on the ground with your back to the mat), as well as the eight positions of power, submission holds, and escape moves. You also take a look at a few of the animals whose natural fighting styles have spawned MMA moves you can add to your repertoire.

Part IV: Becoming a Well-Rounded Fighter — And Person

Becoming a better fighter equates to becoming a more well-rounded individual. Chapter 12 introduces you to critical topics that require the utmost discipline, such as nutrition, flexibility, strength, endurance, mental training, and rest. Chapter 13 helps you hone your skills with fight-specific training drills and games.

Part V: The Part of Tens

Ahh yes — the iconic Part of Tens that appears in each and every *For Dummies* book. Here I provide you with helpful tips on specific aspects of MMA, such as how to improve your speed, how to avoid injuring yourself, and how to prepare for a fight.

Icons Used in This Book

This handy icon points out the tidbits of info that are helpful to keep in mind as you go about your MMA training.

Keep an eye out for this icon to access pointers and recommendations that can make your transition to an MMA way of life a bit easier.

To train in MMA the right way means to keep safety first at all times. This icon is here to keep you from hurting yourself (or someone else!) as you go about your MMA training.

Where to Go from Here

This book is designed so you can start reading anywhere. Take a look at the Table of Contents to see where you want to start, or just take it from the top with Chapter 1 for an overview of MMA. If you want to work on your stand-up fighting, I suggest starting with Chapter 4. On the other hand, if you'd rather practice some submissions, flip to Chapter 9. Wherever you go, your journey into MMA will be a rich one. See you in the cage!

Part I
Welcome to My World (Of Pain)

In this part . . .

Welcome to the world of mixed martial arts, perhaps more commonly known as MMA. More than just a sport or an art, MMA is a way of life that focuses on respecting your knowledge and skills and sharing them with others. These chapters introduce you to the history of MMA, the basics of modern MMA, and the steps you can take to officially begin your MMA training. The part title infers that pain is a part of MMA, and it is, but it's also a sport of pride, discipline, and respect.

Chapter 1

Mixed Martial Arts: Past and Present

In This Chapter

▶ Digging into MMA's roots

▶ Understanding that the art of fighting is the art of living

*M*ixed martial arts (MMA), a lifestyle that focuses on the mixture of martial arts in full-contact combat, has come a long way since I first started practicing the sport in 1994. It can now be found around the globe, from Canada and Brazil to Russia and Japan. It appears on both national and cable television networks in the form of reality programming, sporting leagues, and title championships. Mixed martial artists have become celebrities who star in blockbuster movies, appear as characters in video games, and show up on larger-than-life billboards in some of the biggest cities; some of these stars have even become household names.

With MMA so in the spotlight these days, you may be surprised to know it wasn't always that way. In this chapter, I give you a little insight into MMA's history and introduce you to what MMA is all about as a sport.

From Olympia to America: MMA Reborn as an American Martial Art

The earliest known form of MMA can be traced back to the Olympics of ancient Greece. This hand-to-hand combat performed as a sport was called *pankration,* which comes from the Greek words *pan* and *kratos* and means "all powers." The competitors had only two rules to abide by: no biting and no eye gouging. Pankration was a popular event, and the competitors became heroes and the subjects of legends.

The teachings of pankration spread to India thanks to Alexander the Great and his habit of recruiting athletes as soldiers because of their strength and combat knowledge. A Buddhist monk traveling through India picked up on aspects of pankration and brought that knowledge to China, where it birthed Asian martial arts such as kung fu, judo, and karate. As people branched into new lands, they took these arts and built on them, often creating a new style or form of martial art. For example, an expert in judo traveled the globe and ended up in Brazil to spread his teachings, an act that gave birth to the art of Brazilian Jiu-Jitsu.

As martial arts spread, so did the idea of mixed-style competitions. Often a practitioner of one martial art challenged a practitioner of a different one for ultimate bragging rights. These mixed-style competitions took place worldwide for several decades, eventually gaining intense popularity in the United States.

Participants in these competitions learned from their opponents and began to realize that in order to become well-rounded fighters, they must study any combative art form that could give them an edge in the game. For instance, if a kickboxer was matched with a Brazilian Jiu-Jitsu practitioner, the kickboxer would realize that he must become more adept at defending takedowns, thus prompting him to train with Brazilian Jiu-Jitsu fighters. From that point forward, competitions were no longer between athletes who focused on a singular martial art but between two mixed martial arts athletes.

The Many Faces of MMA

The sport of MMA exists in many countries around the world under different names. Here's a look at the different forms of MMA from an assortment of cultures:

- **Lucha libre in Mexico:** Spanish for "free wrestling," *lucha libre* is a Mexican form of professional wrestling, but some luchadores perform in MMA competitions.
- **Pankration in Greece:** From the Greek words *pan* and *kratos, pankration* means "all powers," a fitting definition considering Greek fighters could do anything except bite an opponent or gouge his eye.
- **Shooto in Japan:** The combat sport of shoot wrestling (also known as *Shooto* or shoot boxing) originated in Japan.
- **Systema in Russia:** Translating to "the system," *Systema* is the Russian martial art of hand-to-hand combat.
- **Vale tudo in Brazil:** In Portuguese, *vale tudo* means "anything goes," with *vale* meaning "is allowed" and *tudo* meaning "everything." Consequently, any and every move is allowed in a vale tudo bout except biting, eye gouging, and fish hooking.

In the United States, MMA takes the "no holds barred" approach, meaning there's a decided lack of restrictions in hand-to-hand combat competitions. The phrase "no holds barred" has become synonymous with American MMA, which relies on fighting organizations to host *fighting promotions* (events). These groups often have a roster of fighters, as well as their own championship belts and title events. For more on MMA organizations and fighting promotions, see Chapter 2.

Breaking Down the MMA Skill Set

MMA is a mix of many different styles of martial arts, but you can break down the skill sets into two main categories: stand-up fighting and ground fighting.

Stand-up fighting

Stand-up fighting encompasses all fighting done while standing. Punches, kicks, knee-and-elbow moves, and *takedowns* (moving your opponent to the ground from a standing position) are all a part of stand-up fighting. Some of the fighting styles used in stand-up are western boxing, Muay Thai, and American kickboxing. Part II of this book delves into the various aspects of stand-up fighting.

Ground fighting

Ground fighting consists of engaging from positions like the guard and the mount, strikes from ground-based positions, and *submissions* (obtaining a hold that manipulates your opponent's joints in the hopes that he'll remove himself from the fight due to pain or fear of injury). Two of the fighting styles used in ground fighting are Brazilian Jiu-Jitsu and wrestling. Part III of this book introduces you to the ground game.

Setting Training Goals

What do you want to accomplish by practicing MMA? If you look at MMA as a fun way to keep in shape, you'll have different goals than someone who wants to fight in a professional bout. That's perfectly okay, so long as you set goals for yourself.

After you know what you want to accomplish, stay focused in your training by setting small goals each week. Smaller goals are easier to reach, and accomplishing these goals builds self-confidence and feeds your drive to succeed.

If you want to become a professional fighter, focus one week on perfecting a specific submission hold (like those presented in Chapter 9). The next week you can turn your attention to a specific takedown (see Chapter 6), and the week after that you can work on a specific training game (see Chapter 13). If you just want a fun way to stay in shape, you can focus on a goal like the amount of time you can last in a sparring session. Try sparring with a partner for five minutes and build the number of rounds each week.

I cover training — both mental and physical — in Chapters 12 and 13.

The Shamrock Way: The Art of Fighting Is the Art of Living

My fighting philosophy, which I call the *Shamrock Way,* centers on the idea that the art of fighting is the art of living a rich, fulfilled life. A key tenet of the Shamrock Way is that you must be honest with yourself and others. In doing so, you strengthen your spirit and the spirits of those around you.

In addition to being truthful, following the Shamrock Way means you should join a community, serve a greater cause, and embrace humility. Many MMA communities serve the greater cause by working with the community at large. For example, at my schools, I offer training to underprivileged young men and veterans. Often members of my schools run together in marathons benefiting nonprofit organizations.

Being part of an MMA community also teaches you humility. After all, studying MMA means admitting you're not an expert. Humility also comes into play when working with partners. If your partner obtains a submission hold on you, you must respect yourself and your partner by admitting that he has won. Embracing humility allows you to learn at the best of your ability and grow exponentially as a fighter and a person.

The plus sign (+), equal sign (=), and minus sign (–) represent the core of the Shamrock Way: the three people you need to make you the best you can be.

- ✔ The plus sign represents the one person who knows more than you and has better skills in order to teach you what you need to learn.
- ✔ The equal sign represents the one person who has equal knowledge and skill to spar with you.
- ✔ The minus sign represents the one person who knows less than you and can help you test your knowledge.

You can certainly train at MMA on your own, but if you want to grow your skills, training with others and finding a solid MMA community (such as a school or gym) is the best way to go. When searching for that community, be aware of the people training there and see whether they have the potential to be one of these three kinds of people for you. Finding training partners and friends is a rewarding experience for all involved.

The Shamrock Way is derived from Bushido, which means "way of the warrior." *Bushido* was the ancient code of the samurai; it directed the warriors to live their lives respectably, honestly, and morally.

Respecting and Sharing Your New Power

Studying and practicing MMA gives you knowledge of dangerous and powerful techniques that most people you encounter won't have. Respect yourself and others by using your new knowledge and skills appropriately and sharing them in the proper venues and situations, as explained in the following sections.

Choosing the right path

You ultimately have to choose whether to use your knowledge and skills for good or for bad. On the good side, you can choose to maintain a healthy lifestyle and share what you know by, say, teaching a family member self-defense techniques. Or you can go down the bad path and act like a bully, intimidate people, and get into bar fights.

If you want to be a true mixed martial artist, don't abuse your knowledge. Instead, show your humility by applying your skills in the right situations, not when you have something to gain.

Treating your body well

How you treat your body directly affects both your MMA training and your life. Always protect your body. When training, wear the right protective gear and work under the supervision of a skilled instructor. Plan a training schedule and stick to it. In your personal life, be sure to eat enough fruits and vegetables, drink enough water, and get enough sleep. Always, always listen to your body and never train if you're feeling tired or hurt. (Flip to Chapter 12 for specific recommendations regarding nutrition, hydration, and rest.)

Getting involved in an MMA community

Being a part of a community is essential, so you should work to find others with similar interests. After all, staying on a desired path is easier when you have friends and supporters by your side. The good news is you can form the foundation for a community with just one other person (although ideally your community should have the three people who can help you be a better person and fighter, as described earlier in this chapter). I provide you with specific tips on finding a good instructor and gym in Chapter 3.

Chapter 2

Digging Deeper into MMA

Mixed martial arts (MMA) is exactly what it sounds like: a form of martial arts that incorporates a variety of different fighting styles. Some of these influences may surprise you. For instance, would you believe that collegiate wrestling helped mold the MMA of today? (Fortunately it didn't have an impact on MMA attire.) Here, I introduce you to the fighting styles that have influenced modern MMA. I also get you up to speed on the rules of the sport and explain all that MMA does for you (just in case you need to defend your pursuit of it to a parent, spouse, or significant other who doesn't share your enthusiasm).

MMA Fighting Styles

MMA can be a mixture of any combative art, but here are some prominent fighting styles that have helped make MMA what it is today:

- ✔ **Brazilian Jiu-Jitsu:** The guard position (shown in Chapter 7) and many of the various submission holds (presented in Chapter 9) come from Brazilian Jiu-Jitsu.

- ✔ **Collegiate wrestling:** Clinches (Chapter 5) and takedowns (Chapter 6) entered the MMA repertoire thanks to collegiate wrestling.

- ✔ **Judo:** The hip toss (Chapter 6) and other throws are judo's gift to MMA.

- ✔ **Muay Thai:** Kicks, as well as knee-and-elbow moves, in MMA are attributed to Muay Thai. (Check out Chapter 4 for details on these moves.)

- ✔ **Submission wrestling:** Position flows (Chapter 8) and submission combinations (Chapter 9) come from submission wrestling.

- ✔ **Western boxing:** The strikes used in MMA (see Chapter 4) may look familiar if you've ever watched a traditional western boxing match.

I've taken aspects of each of these fighting styles to mold my own fighting style that I call submission fighting. Specifically, my personal fighting style incorporates wrestling, boxing, Muay Thai, judo, and Jiu-Jitsu. I've become a well-rounded MMA fighter by studying every combative martial art and teaching those arts to others. Become a well-rounded fighter yourself by finding out as much as you can and sharing your knowledge with others.

The Rules of the Game

The rules of MMA differ slightly from one promotion to the next because each fighting organization can create unique rules. For example, the rules for the UFC may differ slightly from the rules for Strikeforce. However, every event must comply with the athletic commission rules of the state in which the event is being held.

Athletic commissions from several states created the *Unified Rules of Mixed Martial Arts,* a set of rules that have been adopted by fighting promotions worldwide. These rules are the most widely used rules for MMA. For a complete listing of them, please refer to the aforementioned document, available online at www.nj.gov/lps/sacb/docs/martial.html.

Weight classes

No matter where you're fighting, one of the most basic rules of MMA is that you must fight within your weight class. For instance, a male lightweight who weighs 150 pounds would never be matched with a male heavyweight who weighs 240 pounds. That kind of pairing is saved solely for cartoons. ***Note:*** If you don't make weight for a match, you can be disqualified and possibly fined by the promotion. See Tables 2-1 and 2-2 for a rundown of the specific weight classes defined in the *Unified Rules of MMA.*

Table 2-1	MMA Weight Classes for Men
Class	*Weight Range*
Flyweight	Up to 105 lbs
Super flyweight	105.1–115 lbs
Bantamweight	115.1–125 lbs
Super bantamweight	125.1–135 lbs
Featherweight	135.1–145 lbs
Lightweight	145.1–155 lbs
Super lightweight	155.1–165 lbs
Welterweight	165.1–175 lbs
Super welterweight	175.1–185 lbs
Middleweight	185.1–195 lbs
Super middleweight	195.1–205 lbs
Light heavyweight	205.1–225 lbs
Heavyweight	225.1–265 lbs
Super heavyweight	Over 265 lbs

Table 2-2	MMA Weight Classes for Women
Class	*Weight Range*
Flyweight	Up to 95 lbs
Bantamweight	95.1–105 lbs
Featherweight	105.1–115 lbs
Lightweight	115.1–125 lbs
Welterweight	125.1–135 lbs
Middleweight	135.1–145 lbs
Light heavyweight	145.1–155 lbs
Cruiserweight	155.1–165 lbs
Heavyweight	165.1–185 lbs
Super heavyweight	Over 185 lbs

MMA no-no's

Although every MMA fighting organization has its own specific rules, some universal no-no's do exist. They're listed in the *Unified Rules of MMA,* but here's a quick look at what's not allowed:

- ✔ No groin attacks.
- ✔ No knees to the head on a grounded opponent.
- ✔ No strikes to the back of the head or the spine.
- ✔ No head butts. (Sorry, soccer fans.)
- ✔ No eye gouging.
- ✔ No fish hooking.
- ✔ No fingers in an opponent's orifices. (Eww!)
- ✔ No biting.
- ✔ No hair pulling. (Besides, that's so second grade.)
- ✔ No strikes or grabbing of the throat.
- ✔ No manipulation of the fingers or toes.
- ✔ No intentional grabbing of the ring or cage.
- ✔ No intentional throwing of your opponent outside of the ring or cage. (That stuff belongs in professional wrestling.)

Accidentally performing one of these actions in a fight earns you an automatic warning from the referee. If your opponent was injured from your accidental action, he'll get five minutes to recover.

Approved ways to end a fight

An MMA match can end in one of several ways:

- ✔ **Decision:** If a fight lasts all rounds, the outcome is decided by three judges. Each fighting promotion has its own unique point system.

- ✔ **Disqualification (DQ):** Think of this as a sort of "three strikes and you're out" policy. Each time a fighter engages in an illegal move, he receives a warning. After three warnings, he's disqualified. A DQ can also be called if a fighter has been injured by an illegal move that seemed intentional.

- ✔ **Forfeit:** A fighter can announce a forfeit before a match begins if he's injured.

- ✔ **Knockout (KO):** A *knockout* is when a fighter loses consciousness thanks to his opponent's strikes.

- ✔ **No contest:** If both fighters violate the rules, or if a fighter is injured by an unintentional illegal action, a no-contest call can result. No contest is rarely called in MMA fights.

- ✔ **Submission:** If one fighter achieves a submission hold, the fighter trapped in the hold can call defeat by tapping out on his opponent's body or the mat, or by making a verbal announcement. Some defeated fighters fail to tap out and become incapacitated. In such cases, the referee calls an end to the fight. (See Chapter 3 for more info on tapping out.)

- ✔ **Technical knockout (TKO):** A *technical knockout,* when a fight is ended by the referee, doctor, or fighter's corner, can be called in a few ways. The referee can call one when a fighter is no longer defending himself, usually due to an effective attack by his opponent. A doctor can also call a TKO if it's clear that continuing the fight could be dangerous. And finally, a fighter's corner can throw in a towel to admit defeat, resulting in a TKO.

Fighting promotions

Fighting promotions are events put on by MMA organizations, and each one has its own rules and regulations. Although most fighting promotions use the rules outlined in the *Unified Rules of MMA,* the length of rounds, number of rounds, and rest period in between all differ by organization. Additionally, attire, fouls, conduct, and judging criteria can all be defined under each organization's regulations.

There are, however, some common elements. Generally fight rounds last five minutes; three rounds make up a match, unless you're participating in a championship match, which can last for five rounds. The various promotions usually restrict fighting attire to approved fight shorts for men and women, a sports bra or top for women, and light gloves for men and women that allow for finger movement.

Following are some of the fighting promotions currently active in the U.S.:

- ✔ **Ultimate Fighting Championship:** In the same way people call cotton swabs by the brand name "Q-Tips," MMA is often called by the brand name "UFC" or "ultimate fighting." Currently the most successful fighting promotion in the world, the UFC gained popularity through its presence on SPIKE TV and Pay-Per-View (PPV).

- ✔ **Strikeforce:** Based in San Jose, California, Strikeforce has aired its fights on NBC, SHOWTIME, and ESPN.

- ✔ **Affliction:** A new promotion founded in 2008, Affliction has had two events aired on PPV and HDNet Fights.

- ✔ **King of the Cage:** Founded in 1998, King of the Cage has remained a steady promotion with a reputation of finding and building MMA talent. Many KOTC fighters go on to become UFC Champions.

Each fighting promotion has its own patented or trademarked rings or cages. Promotions try to come up with something gimmicky or new to get people to watch their events. That's why you may have noticed that UFC fights take place in the Octagon, Strikeforce fights occur in a six-sided cage, and Affliction fights use a traditional boxing ring. The *Unified Rules of MMA* lists requirements for the fighting area that promotions must abide by.

If you're interested in fighting professionally, start with where you train. After you've sparred with other students from your school, you can test your skills by competing in smoker events. A *smoker event* is when members of one MMA school compete against members of another MMA school in exhibition bouts where there are no losers and no winners. If you're interested in smoker events, it's best to ask potential schools whether they participate in them. See Chapter 3 for help finding a good school.

The Benefits of MMA

Perhaps you're gung-ho and ready to begin your MMA training, but your loved ones are holding you back or trying to dampen your interest. They may equate MMA only with fighting and not with the vast and diverse benefits it provides to those who study it. Share this list of life-changing benefits the next time someone asks you why you want to get involved in MMA:

- ✔ **Community:** Joining an MMA community keeps you on track with your training and helps you make some friends along the way.

- ✔ **Confidence:** The confidence built from training in MMA can accompany you into the office, your relationships, and wherever else you can use a self-assurance boost! You may find yourself with increased leadership skills or an ability to conquer presentations just like you would in the ring. Your newfound confidence will also help deter any would-be attackers.

- ✔ **Discipline:** The discipline you're sure to develop from training in MMA can be applied to the rest of your life, from enhancing your capacity to stick to a schedule to strengthening your resolve to eat well.

- ✔ **Fitness:** Training in MMA is guaranteed to improve your level of fitness. MMA fighters are some of the most superior, well-rounded, Olympic-caliber athletes of the day. Living the MMA lifestyle can therefore transform your body, along with your mind and spirit.

- ✔ **Self-defense:** Studying MMA can greatly increase your level of preparedness in the face of a dangerous situation. With your knowledge of combative arts, you can defend yourself whenever you need to.

Chapter 3

Getting Started with Your Training

As soon as you decide to live in a martial way and commit yourself to a higher cause, you'll see immediate physical, psychological, and spiritual results, such as a stronger body, enhanced confidence, and a healthier mind. But first you have to develop good, safe training habits. You don't want to injure yourself or others when you train — that's why practicing under the supervision of a qualified instructor is so important. Developing bad technique will result in injury, but learning good technique from a skilled instructor will keep you safe. In this chapter, I show you how to keep your body in shape so you're not prone to injury. I also introduce you to the equipment you need to protect yourself and help you find a good instructor.

Getting in Touch with Your Animal Instincts

Tuning in to your animal instincts can help you as you work to strengthen your MMA skills. After all, animals are the most primitive of fighters, and each one has its own unique strategy for attacking or defending. Following are the animal fighting styles that will help you in your MMA ground-fighting game (I cover them in detail in Chapter 11):

✔ The turtle

✔ The dog

✔ The cat

✔ The snake

✔ The monkey

Conditioning and Stretching Your Body

If you want to improve your chances of successfully avoiding injury, conditioning and stretching your body is extremely important. Think of your body as a machine that needs to be kept in tip-top shape to achieve the best performance — which is precisely where conditioning comes in. Conditioning prepares your body for a variety of activities.

Just starting out and not quite in shape yet? Don't do more than 30 minutes of conditioning a day. If you can't go for 30 minutes right off the bat, that's okay. Work up to this ideal gradually and keep listening to your body so you know when you're rocking it and when you're overdoing it.

Aim to condition your body for 30 minutes a day, three days a week. Gradually build yourself up to working out for one hour a day, four days a week. Maintain a steady workout schedule no matter how experienced an MMA fighter you become.

Keeping your body flexible and elastic is but a close second to keeping it conditioned. The more you train in MMA, the more you need to stretch. As a beginner, be sure to stretch the core areas you'll be targeting with your training. As you progress, you'll need to stretch even more because you'll be using more areas of your body as you train. See Chapter 12 for more on specific conditioning and stretching tips.

Focusing Your Mind through Meditation

When the machine of your body is prepared through conditioning and stretching (as described in the preceding section), you need to focus and program it through meditation. Meditation strengthens the most important part of your body — the brain. I recommend meditating at least twice a day, once in the morning and once at night. If you're new to meditating, it's surprisingly easier than you may think. Just relax, breathe, and think positive.

Meditation can also help you in training and competition. The practice of breathing deeply and clearing your mind can keep you focused when you're getting fatigued. So instead of getting scared when your opponent traps you in a bad position, just breathe, clear any fear you have in your mind, and focus on what you want to accomplish, such as getting into a better position. I offer further guidance on focusing your mind in Chapter 12.

Understanding the Concepts of Combat

Sure, MMA training teaches you how to punch and kick your way to a victory, but all the specialized techniques in the world aren't going to make you successful if you don't enter your MMA training with a basic understanding of the concepts of combat. Review the following list (which starts with the most important concepts) and refer back to it whenever you wonder why your instructor is asking you to do something a certain way:

- ✔ Protect yourself at all times.
- ✔ Always aim to inflict the most amount of damage to your opponent with the least amount of effort and damage to yourself.
- ✔ Your weight is your greatest weapon in *grappling* (ground fighting).
- ✔ Speed equals power. Can you think of any good MMA fighters who can be described as slow? Me either. That's because there aren't any. Good fighters are quick fighters.
- ✔ Angles are important: Position yourself at 90 degrees from your opponent for strength and 45 degrees from your opponent for speed. Flip to Chapter 8 to see angles used in specific positions.

✔ Every movement is followed by either a reaction to the movement or a counter to the movement. Constantly moving is a great way to create energy and confuse your opponent.

✔ Focused breath is what gives you explosive power. Begin each and every exertion with a full, focused release of your breath.

Knowing How to Protect Yourself (Even If That Means Tapping)

Protecting yourself and your peers is a core component of good MMA training, whether you're a beginner or a pro. The best thing you can do is be watchful. Never take your eyes off of your opponent. Be present and aware during each movement.

Tapping — the act of tapping an opponent anywhere on the body or the mat, or a verbal request to end the match — offers another method of protection. When your opponent has control of your body (like when you're in a submission hold; I present the various submission holds in Chapter 9), tap if you feel pain or discomfort. And contrary to what some folks believe, tapping isn't dishonorable — it's smart.

Stay in constant communication with your training partner to avoid injury. If you can't reach his body for a tap, tap the mat loudly or say something. Even though you're giving up the hold, you're not giving up the fight. Protect yourself and show respect to your training partner by communicating that the hold is successful.

Gathering the Necessary Training Equipment

Like any sport, MMA requires you to have special equipment, largely for keeping yourself protected during your training sessions. Here are some of the important supplies and gear you should gather before starting your MMA training:

✔ **Boxing gloves:** Essential for working on strikes.

✔ **Handwraps:** Good for protecting your hands when training or fighting competitively.

✔ **Headgear:** Used for sparring to protect the skull from harsh blows.

✔ **Cup:** Essential for male MMA fighters.

✔ **Mouthpiece:** Essential for protecting your teeth while competing and training. Try conditioning while wearing a mouthpiece to get used to wearing one.

✔ **MMA gloves:** Necessary for competitions. I suggest wearing them during sparring and grappling sessions as well so you can get accustomed to them.

✔ **MMA shin guards:** Helpful for protecting your shins when training or sparring.

✔ **Stability ball:** A great tool for working on your balance and control. I provide tips and suggestions for ball training in Chapter 13.

✔ **Jump rope:** Useful for warming up before training and a common tool for MMA practitioners.

✔ **Thai pads and focus mitts:** Good for using with a partner when you want to work on knees, kicks, and other strikes.

✔ **Kettlebells:** One of my favorite tools for full-body conditioning.

✔ **MMA attire:** Can be worn inside and outside of the ring and includes T-shirts, hoodies, sweats, and shorts. MMA attire tells people that you're living the MMA lifestyle. It's a conversation starter, and it may just stop someone from trying to push you around and steal your milk money.

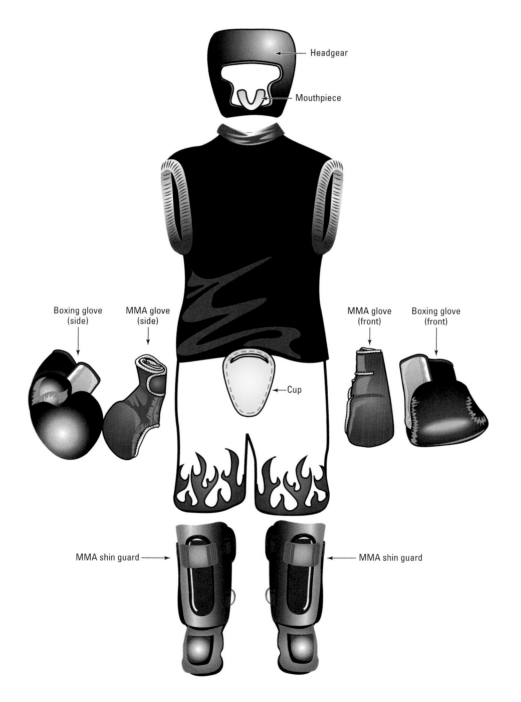

Most gyms specializing in MMA will have a lot of this equipment. As for schools, they usually suggest that you buy your own handwraps, mouthpiece, cup, and gloves. Look to see whether a school you're interested in has some of the listed equipment available. A good school or gym has plenty of MMA gear and safety equipment (think mats and first aid kits).

Finding a Good Training Facility and a Qualified Instructor

The gym or school where you train is the foundation of the MMA community you're going to build for yourself, and your instructor is the person who can share his knowledge and help you grow your skills. To find the right gym or school for you, you need to consider your own needs and requirements. Factors such as cost, class times, and the number of students can all have an impact on your decision. Other factors, such as cleanliness, space, and safety are also valuable to consider, but they usually play a smaller role in the decision-making process than your personal needs and requirements.

If you want to make the process of finding a good gym or school easier, make sure to identify and set your MMA training goals prior to beginning your search. (Flip to Chapter 1 for goal-setting help.)

In addition to finding the right training facility, you need to find a qualified MMA instructor who can teach you and supervise your training sessions. Certifications aren't available for MMA instructors, but there are professional groups such as the National Association of Professional Martial Artists (NAPMA) and the Martial Arts Teachers Association (MATA). Check to see whether your potential instructor is a member of either group and whether he has insurance.

Don't worry if a potential instructor doesn't have belts and trophies covering his walls. Whether an instructor has competed professionally is really a nonissue. In fact, some professional fighters aren't the best instructors.

Most MMA schools welcome visitors and may even offer a free class. Dropping by or participating in a free training session is a great way to check out the facility, the MMA community within it, and the instructor. If you're not sure where to begin your search, start with the phone book and look up MMA schools in your area, or get on the Internet. Web sites such as Yelp.com may have some useful user reviews on MMA schools in your area. You can also visit MMA forums and community Web sites where users connect with other MMA fans and practitioners to offer advice and resources.

Take your time to research and find the best training facility and instructor for you. Also, don't forget to look at the community within that facility. You need one person who knows more than you, one who's equal with you, and one who knows less than you so you can grow by interacting with each person (as explained in Chapter 1).

Part II
Stand-Up Fighting

In this part . . .

A core aspect of MMA is stand-up fighting, which involves striking your opponent while standing, fighting inside the clinch, and taking your opponent down. In this part, I walk you through how to add these various stand-up fighting techniques to your repertoire.

Chapter 4

Stand Up for Yourself and Strike

. . . .

In This Chapter

▶ Finding a centered fighting stance

▶ Practicing specific strikes and combinations

▶ Blocking your opponent's strikes

. . . .

*N*ow more than ever before in the history of the sport, stand-up fighting in mixed mar-tial arts (MMA) has become paramount. Because of the newfound popularity of the sport and its presence on television, rules under different MMA promotions have changed in favor of keeping bouts standing. If you watch enough MMA, you'll often see referees stop a fight when the participants have become inactive on the ground in order to get them standing again. A strong base in stand-up fighting will give you the confidence you need to see a fight to the finish.

In this chapter, I help you work on your stand-up game by showing you how to perfect a cen-tered fighting stance, covering all the basic strikes and combinations, and demonstrating some standard defensive moves.

Core Position: Fighting Stance

You're not going to fight effectively without a solid stance. Here are the key components to a good stance for stand-up fighting:

✔ **Surfing stance:** A good fighting stance looks almost like you're surfing. Your body is sideways, and your legs are bent.

✔ **Heel on the line, toe on the line:** Imagine a line that runs down the center of your body. The line should hit the heel of your back foot and the toe of your front foot.

✔ **Hands up, elbows in, chin down:** Both of your hands should be up, protecting your face. Your front hand should be out in front, and your dominant hand should be under-neath your chin. (For most people, the right hand is the dominant one because they're right-handed. If you're left-handed, your dominant hand is your left hand.) Protect your chin by keeping it down and keep your elbows pointed inward.

✔ **Breathe before every strike and counterstrike:** Breathing focuses your energy.

✔ **Stay at eye level with your opponent:** Always stay at eye level with your opponent. If he changes levels, change your level as well. When you're at his level, you can recognize when he's about to attempt a takedown or strike so you can counter accordingly.

✔ **Centered and balanced position:** You must be centered and balanced in your fighting stance so you can be ready for both offense and defense.

Focusing on the T-zone

The *T-zone* includes the chin, nose, and temples and represents the most fragile areas of the face. A punch to the jaw could shake your brain and shut your body down, knocking you unconscious. Use this knowledge to your advantage by protecting your own T-zone and striving to strike your opponent's.

Keep those hands up. How else are you going to protect your face?

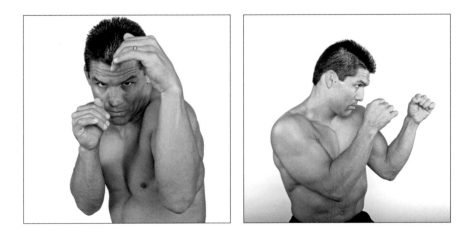

Aim for your opponent's T-zone. Think of your opponent's T-zone as a power switch to his body. If you hit that switch just right, it's lights out for your opponent. So always aim for your opponent's T-zone when striking — whether from a standing position or on the ground. And try to strike with the two knuckles outlined below.

Using your clock to achieve power

Distance in stand-up fighting is the key ingredient for generating power. With distance, you can pivot, twist, rotate, step, and swing to get that extra power. Without distance, you're forced to defend yourself without the space you need for a powerful countermove.

Imagine that you're standing on a clock. Your opponent should always remain in front of you at 12 o'clock. To attack safely and with maximum power, be sure to do the following:

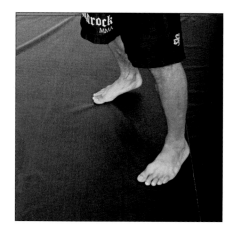

1. **Maintain a centered and balanced fighting stance.**

   Here, you can see my feet lined up for an opponent at 12 o' clock.

2. **Now step to a new time on your clock (either 10 or 2 o'clock) and strike.**

   Entering this new *time zone,* or angle, moves your body and head out of your opponent's line of fire and allows you to strike without being hit.

When you step into a new time zone, you create a new center for your body, so be sure to step into your new time zone and immediately regain a solid, centered fighting stance before striking your opponent.

Punching Your Way to Victory

A punch is usually the first type of move a fighter uses in a fight. It's also the most commonly used type of strike in MMA competitions. A strong knowledge of punches and how to defend against them can give you the upper hand in any bout that starts with the fighters standing up.

Jab

A *jab,* also known as a *straight,* is the first strike used in most punching combinations. It's a fast punch that distracts your opponent from the next strike to come.

1. **First, maintain a good fighting stance.**

   Here, you can see both fighters in the proper stance with their arms up.

2. **Step a little forward as you extend palm down, knuckles forward.**

3. **As you fully extend your jab, move your head a little out of the way so it's not in line with your opponent's punch.**

   By moving your head, you position your body in a new *time zone* (angle) so that your head isn't in line with your opponent's punch. For more on using your clock, see the related section earlier in this chapter.

4. **Keep your other hand up to protect your face.**

   After all, what's the point of striking if you leave yourself open to attack?

5. **Return to fighting stance.**

Front uppercut

The *front uppercut* is an effective strike when you have a small amount of distance between you and your opponent.

1. **Keep your hands up to protect your face.**

   In this case, I've ducked in anticipation of my sparring partner's jab.

2. **Strike with your front arm. Use your legs to lift and punch up.**

   Your palm faces you as you strike at your opponent's center.

3. **Keep your other hand up to protect your face.**

4. **Return to fighting stance.**

Rear uppercut

The *rear uppercut* is a powerful strike that can be devastating to your opponent. It's also a good strike to use when you're in close quarters with your opponent.

1. **Keep your hands up to protect your face.**

   Again, I've moved lower in preparation for an uppercut.

2. **Use your rear arm to reach toward the ceiling and punch your opponent.**

3. **Lift your heel and hip as you pivot and rotate into the uppercut.**

   Using your legs adds power to your strike.

4. **Return to fighting stance.**

Cross

The *cross* is a punch that's just like the jab except it comes from across the body.

1. **From your fighting stance, punch with your dominant hand.**

2. **As you extend, twist your hip forward, raise your back heel, and pivot with the punch, keeping your other hand up to protect your face.**

   Even when you're on the offensive, you should never knowingly leave yourself open to attack.

3. **Return to fighting stance.**

Hook

Throwing a hook means exposing the front side of your body. Consequently, maintaining good technique is essential during this move. Follow these steps and you'll be set.

1. **From a good fighting stance, prepare to punch from the side with the hand you jab with.**

   Your arm should be parallel to the ground with your palm down and your knuckles toward your opponent. Whichever arm you use, that side of your body should twist with the punch.

2. **Raise your foot and pivot with the punch, keeping your other hand up to protect your face.**

3. **Return to fighting stance.**

Kicking with Variety

Kicks are some of the most powerful strikes you can use, and the results can be devastating. I should know — I broke my opponent's arm in my kickboxing debut.

Switch kick

A switch kick is best used in combination with other strikes. The setup for the kick takes some time, which can give your opponent more of an opportunity to see the kick coming and check it. Yet with practice, the switch kick can be effective because switching your legs can throw off your opponent.

1. **From a strong fighting stance, shuffle your rear leg to 2 o'clock while your front hand blocks your opponent's face.**

   Protect your face with your other arm.

2. **Kick with your front leg by spinning on the ball of your foot and rotating your hips.**

   Be quick and make sure your hand remains up to protect your face.

3. **Return to fighting stance.**

Inside out kick

The way you replace your legs for the inside out kick can catch your opponent unawares.

1. **From your fighting stance, lean back to protect your head.**

   Bringing your hand up also serves to block your opponent's face.

2. **Bend your back knee as you lean back and prepare to strike.**

3. **Kick with your front leg so that the bottom of your shin hits the inside of your opponent's knee.**

4. **Return to fighting stance.**

Front leg roundhouse kick

Roundhouse kicks are the most powerful and effective of all the kicks you can possibly use. The front leg roundhouse kick is less powerful than the rear leg roundhouse kick (described in the next section), but it's great to use in combinations.

1. **From a good fighting stance, step to 2 o'clock with your rear leg.**

2. **Spin on the ball of your foot and kick with your front leg, bringing your front hand up for balance and to block your opponent's face.**

   If you don't bring your front hand up, the momentum of your movement may cause you to fall.

Your shin is what makes contact with your opponent. Be sure to drive through with your hips and bring the knee across the body.

3. **Return to fighting stance.**

Rear leg roundhouse kick

The most powerful of all the kicks, the *rear leg roundhouse kick* offers more room for your hips to rotate and add momentum to your strike.

1. **From a strong fighting stance, step to 10 o'clock with your front leg.**

   Step like you're going to wak in that direction.

2. **Raise your front hand for balance and to block your opponent's face.**

3. **Spin on the ball of your front foot and kick with your rear leg.**

   Your shin is what connects with your opponent.

4. **Return to fighting stance.**

Front kick with front leg

The *front kick with front leg* is a good kick to employ for keeping your opponent at bay and at a safe distance away from your body.

1. **From your fighting stance, lift your front leg and push the ball of your foot into your opponent's midsection or front leg.**

   Drive your hips through the strike.

2. **Return to fighting stance.**

You can also perform a front kick with your rear leg if you have the time and space. Kicking with your rear leg gives your front kick more power than if you kick with your front leg. The energy of your hips is actually the driving force behind this strike.

Springing Your Knee on a Nearby Opponent

Using your knee effectively in stand-up fighting requires a closed distance. Knee strikes are usually only done as a countermove, in combinations, or within the clinch position (described in Chapter 5). Here, I show you the rear and front knee strikes in the context of a striking opponent who has just closed the distance.

Rear knee

The *rear knee* is one of the most devastating strikes in MMA. All the momentum for it comes directly from your hips.

1. **Step to 10 o'clock.**

   In this case, I'm fighting off a punch from my sparring partner, so I step toward 10 o'clock and use my hand to protect my face.

2. **Lift your rear leg and hip and use your knee to strike your opponent's body. Point your toes down to relax your hip, which enables you to knee higher.**

   Aim for the midsection for the best effect.

3. **Return to fighting stance.**

Front knee

The front knee strike can be used more quickly than the rear knee strike (described in the preceding section) because you have less distance to cover. However, this very fact makes it a less powerful move than the rear knee.

1. **Step to either 10 or 2 o'clock.**

   My sparring partner has moved to throw a jab, so I've stepped to 10 o'clock.

2. **Lift your front leg and hip so your knee can connect with your opponent's body.**

3. **Don't forget to protect your face, like I'm doing here.**

4. **Return to fighting stance.**

Throwing an Elbow

Fighting with your elbow is a technique for closed distances. In the next two sections, you find out the difference between a rear elbow strike and a front elbow strike. Both strikes are presented in the context of an opponent who has just closed the distance.

Rear elbow

The *rear elbow* is a power strike that uses the momentum from your rotating hips to drive your rear elbow into your opponent. The goal? To inflict ultimate damage and possibly cut your opponent.

1. **Step to 10 o'clock.**

   Here, I'm stepping to avoid a right hook.

2. **Lift your rear elbow with your palm facing down and your hand close to your chest.**

3. **Raise your heel and hip and pivot with your elbow as you use it to strike your opponent's head.**

   Pivoting gives your strike extra power.

4. **Return to fighting stance.**

Front elbow

The *front elbow* is a quick strike that inflicts less damage than the rear elbow. It's best used in combinations (which I describe later in this chapter).

1. **Step to 2 o'clock.**

   I'm trying to avoid a jab from my opponent by parrying the punch.

2. **Lift your front elbow with your palm facing down and your hand close to your chest.**

3. **Raise your heel and hip and pivot with your elbow as you use it to strike your opponent's head.**

   This is an important step to ensure you're striking as powerfully as possible.

4. **Return to fighting stance.**

Getting Fancy: Combinations

Combinations are a bit more advanced because they require the knowledge of various strikes and the ability to weave them together into a singular move. If you're up to speed on all the basic strikes, then read on. Otherwise, skip back to the earlier sections in this chapter for a refresher on the particular strike you're unsure of.

Jab cross hook

The *jab cross hook* is a popular and widely used combination.

1. **From a good fighting stance, step forward a little as you extend your front hand, palm down and knuckles forward.**

2. **As you fully extend your jab, move your head a little out of the way so it's not in the same time zone as your opponent's punch and keep your other hand up to protect your face.**

3. **Punch with your dominant hand; as you extend, twist your hip forward, raise your back heel, and pivot with the punch, keeping your other hand up to protect your face.**

4. Use your front arm to punch your opponent from the side while raising your front foot and pivoting with the punch.

5. Return to fighting stance.

Jab uppercut

Throwing a jab before an uppercut can distract your opponent so he won't see your uppercut coming.

1. Use your front arm to jab your opponent.

Try to make contact with your opponent's T-zone. (For more on the T-zone, see "Focusing on the T-zone" earlier in this chapter.

2. Reach your rear arm up toward the ceiling with your palm turned toward your chest and strike your opponent under the chin.

3. Return to fighting stance.

Jab cross hook uppercut

Adding the uppercut to the jab cross hook combination makes for a far more powerful move.

1. **Use your front arm to jab your opponent.**

   Bend your knees for more power.

2. **Use your rear arm to cross punch your opponent.**

   Both your heel and hip rotate with your cross punch to your opponent's T-zone.

3. Use your front arm to punch your opponent's head from the side.

Rotate on the ball of your front foot for power.

4. Use your rear arm to strike your opponent up the center with an uppercut.

You can gain energy with your rear leg by rising to the ball of your foot with your punch.

Keep your chin down, especially on combinations.

5. Return to fighting stance and keep your opponent at 12 o'clock.

Jab roundhouse

Jabbing before you roundhouse kick makes your opponent think more hand strikes will be coming, when in fact your next move is a kick. The advantage? You.

1. **From your fighting stance, step forward a little as you extend your front hand, palm down and knuckles forward.**

2. **As you fully extend your jab, move your head a bit out of the way so it's not in the same time zone as the punch and keep your other hand up to protect your face.**

   Protecting yourself is paramount, even when you're on the offensive.

3. **Pivot on the ball of your front foot and kick with your rear leg, bringing your front hand up for balance and to block your opponent's face.**

   Your shin is your striking point during this maneuver. Aim to hit your opponent's midsection.

4. Return to fighting stance and keep your opponent at 12 o'clock.

Jab hook knee

This combo is guaranteed to surprise your opponent and inflict damage in the process.

1. From a strong fighting stance, use your front arm to jab your opponent.

2. With the same arm, punch your opponent's head from the side by turning your hip and knee and rotating your foot.

3. Lift your front leg and hip so your knee can strike firmly into your opponent's body.

4. Return to fighting stance.

Defending against Strikes

Striking your opponent is only half the fun. You have to be able to block and avoid strikes as well. After all, have you ever played a fighting video game where you can press the back button to block attacks? If you knew to press the back button, you lasted longer and your energy didn't deplete. Of course, fighting in real life isn't as easy as pressing a button, but the same idea applies because defending yourself saves you from getting really hurt and losing a match. That's why I recommend spending half of your training time on defense.

The following sections cover defensive moves such as parrying, blocking, catching, and checking punches and kicks. Clinching is another effective form of defense in MMA fighting, and it's covered in Chapter 5, along with other techniques.

Parrying/catching a punch

A good punch parry is like a windshield wiper: Your hand moves the punch out of the way and keeps you from getting struck.

1. **You observe that a punch is coming toward you.**

2. **Slap the punch out of the way while moving your head away from the attempted strike.**

   You can also catch punches. Just be sure to keep your catching hand far from your face so you aren't struck when you catch the punch.

Blocking with an elbow

If you have minimal distance between you and your opponent (meaning less than 1 foot), blocking with an elbow is a great way to stop a strike while protecting yourself.

1. **You see a punch coming toward you.**

2. **Move either your rear or front elbow up to cover your face and break your opponent's strike.**

3. **Now counterstrike with punch or kick.**

Checking those kicks

If you want to stay standing, you need to check any kicks that come your way. *Checking a kick* means simply lifting the leg that's about to be kicked so that rather than striking your sensitive inner thigh, your opponent is now kicking your large and strong shin bone.

1. **You see a kick coming toward your front leg.**

2. **Turn your heel to the ball of your foot so that the kick lands on your knee.**

3. **Lift your front leg so it's at a 90-degree angle and your shin is pointing toward the incoming kick.**

Always keep your hands up to block potential strikes.

Chapter 5

Inside Fighting with the Clinch

*T*he *clinch,* a standing grappling position in which opponents are in close proximity to one another, is a common tactic in the world of mixed martial arts (MMA) fighting. It's the go-to place for producing powerful short strikes, controlling your opponent, and generating effective takedowns. In some cases, fighters even use the clinch as a place of rest. If you watch any fight today, you'll likely see the clinch in play — unless of course you're watching traditional boxing. Under these rules, fighting from the clinch is illegal and considered dirty boxing. *Dirty boxing* refers to throwing short punches from the clinch, particularly when holding the back of your opponent's head.

In MMA, dirty boxing is safer than striking for two reasons:

✔ If you have control of your opponent's head, you have control of his body. Consequently, you're the one controlling the fight.

✔ By bringing your opponent close to your body, you stop him from generating 100 percent of his body's natural power.

In this chapter, I show you how perfect clinch techniques keep you in control of your opponent. I also introduce you to the various strikes and escapes you can do from inside the clinch.

Clinch Variations

MMA incorporates a variety of variations of the clinch that come from different fighting styles. Here are just a few:

- ✔ The traditional clinch in Muay Thai is formed with two hands on the back of your opponent's neck with your elbows tight together.

- ✔ In wrestling, a traditional clinch consists of pummeling and underhooking.

- ✔ The best version of the clinch is a combination of the traditional Muay Thai and wrestling clinches. With one hand behind your opponent's head and one hand free, you have the opportunity to control and attack your opponent at the same time. You can pull back to create striking space and then close the space before your opponent can strike you in return.

The Core Position: Clinch Hold

The *clinch hold* position is the foundation of dirty boxing. Much like the fighting stance (described in Chapter 4), the clinch hold is based on maintaining a good center of balance and control. Following are the characteristics of a good clinch hold:

- ✔ **Your body is in a centered, balanced position.** Stand sideways with your legs bent, almost like you're surfing. Pretend a line is running through the center of your body, hitting both the front toe of your front leg and the heel of your back leg.

- ✔ **You're in close proximity to your opponent.** Place your front hand on the back of your opponent's head and hook your dominant hand on his bicep. If you're right-handed, your right hand is your dominant one, and your left hand is your front one. If you're left-handed, the opposite is true.

- ✔ **Your chin is down and your shoulders are up.** Always keep yourself protected this way in the clinch hold.

When in this core position, notice the versatility it offers. You can now decide whether you want to remain fighting in the clinch or leave. I offer guidance for fighting in and exiting the clinch later in this chapter. However, in the following sections I show you some alternative clinch positions.

Neck and elbow position

From the *neck and elbow position,* you can easily strike or attempt takedowns — all while defending against your opponent's techniques. Grip the back of your opponent's neck with your front hand. Then grasp your opponent's arm at the bicep or elbow with your dominant hand.

You can obtain greater control by placing your hand on your opponent's bicep. But be sure to relax your grips. You can react more quickly when you are relaxed.

Double head tie

The *double head tie* is very effective in controlling your opponent. When in this position, you can readily attempt knee strikes. Form the double head tie by gripping the back of your opponent's head with both of your hands, interlocking your fingers, keeping your elbows tucked in toward each other, and pulling your opponent's head down.

Always keep your elbows pressed in to prevent your opponent's counter and defend any uppercuts he may throw.

Shoulder-to-shoulder

The *shoulder-to-shoulder* position is a common neutral clinch position in which fighters attempt to advance into a more dominant clinch position. Reach your left arm under your opponent's arm so that your left shoulder is against your opponent's left shoulder. Then pull your opponent's arm underneath your right armpit so that your front shoulder is against your opponent's front shoulder.

Double underhooks

Double underhooks allow for good control and can be used for a takedown (see Chapter 6). This position is also an easy counter if you're in the shoulder-to-shoulder position (described in the preceding section) when your opponent punches you. Swim your arms inside your opponent's arms and hold his midsection or upper body.

Entering the Clinch

The best way to move into the clinch is with any strike. The following sections cover several options for closing the distance between you and your opponent and establishing the clinch.

Punch

Here's how you can punch your way into a clinch:

1. **Step in and jab your opponent. Aim for the throat and you'll connect with the face.**

   I'm in the basic fighting stance here, and I'm not doing anything to indicate that I may move to the clinch.

2. **Be sure to protect your face with your dominant hand.**

   See Chapter 4 for the basics on the jab. I'm still not giving away that I want to move in for a clinch. I'm maintaining eye level with her.

3. **Grab the back of your opponent's head and his bicep.**

   Relax your grips, keep your chin down, and move in shoulder to shoulder.

Jam

If you don't want to enter the clinch on the offense, you can move in defensively when your opponent strikes you.

1. **Fully protect your face with your arm.**

   Even if you've taken a few strikes and your opponent has the upper hand, maintaining a good defense should be as natural as breathing.

2. Step into your opponent's punch while still protecting your face.

Just make sure you block the punch; you definitely don't want to step into it face first.

3. Grab the back of your opponent's head and arm.

Now you can begin fighting in the clinch.

Fighting in the Clinch

Here are a few rules of thumb to keep in mind when fighting in the clinch:

- ✔ Don't wind up your strikes, or else you'll expose your technique.

- ✔ Focus on short, tight, and accurate strikes. Avoid leaning back or creating energy.

- ✔ Don't change your center to make a strike. Maintain a solid, centered stance at all times. If you must leave the stance to strike, immediately return to a strong, centered stance.

- ✔ Move your way up your opponent's body. For knees and kicks, start low. Aim for your opponent's knees and then move up the body to his head. This way you can attack your opponent's base.

- ✔ Don't worry about slamming your opponent with power strikes. Because you don't have the distance inherent in stand-up fighting, you don't need to rotate or pivot to gain power. You only have to use the weight of your strike as power.

The next few sections present some moves you can use to make the clinch hold work to your advantage.

Head punch

You've got your opponent in a clinch. Why not punch him in the head? Seems logical, right?

1. **From the clinch, release your opponent's arm.**

   Continue to maintain a grip on the back of the head.

2. **Before your opponent can take advantage, quickly use that hand to throw a punch to the face.**

   Return to the clinch immediately.

Uppercut

The uppercut can be a devastating blow if properly unleashed. Here's how to do just that:

1. **Release your opponent's arm and drop your arm below his elbow.**

2. **Turn your palm toward yourself and punch your opponent's chin.**

   Don't wind up your punch. Doing so gives away your move. Punch through the chin towards the sky for maximum power.

3. **After you connect, immediately return to your clinch hold.**

Punch to body

You can wear down your opponent with some body work.

1. Let go of your opponent's arm.

Maintain your grip on the head with your other hand.

2. Punch straight to the body.

If possible, throw multiple punches, but remember that your opponent's left arm is free.

3. Return to the clinch hold position.

Elbow

In close quarters, sometimes throwing an elbow is a better option than a punch.

1. **Release your opponent's bicep.**

   Don't forget to keep your grip on the head.

2. **Bring your elbow up and down the center of your opponent's face, rotating your shoulder and torso as you go.**

   Don't release the head, and push your elbow through the face for more damage.

3. **Return to your clinch hold.**

Knee

With your opponent in close, striking with your knee can be an effective tactic, especially if you can knee him in the head.

1. **Maintain your stance.**

   Keep your eyes up to avoid giving away to your opponent that you're about to throw a knee.

2. **Connect your knee bone to the center of your opponent's muscle, right above his knee.**

   Point your toes down to relax your hip flexor and stay centered.

3. **Return to the clinch hold position.**

You can also kick from the clinch even though you may not think you have room. Just use your rear leg to kick your opponent's front leg in the thigh. Use your leg bones and weight to make contact.

Escaping the Clinch

Say your opponent has you tied up in a clinch. How do you get out? The following sections give you some options.

Shoulder shuck

This move, when done properly, will get you out of the clinch in no time.

1. From the clinch hold position, lift your shoulder to trap your opponent's hand into the hold.

You want the hand caught between your jaw and shoulder.

2. Take your hand from the top of your opponent's arm to the side of his elbow.

3. **Rotate your torso and push your opponent's elbow across his body and toward the ground.**

4. **Return to your fighting stance.**

   Start throwing some punches or kicks.

Duck under

With practice, this simple maneuver can smoothly free you from your opponent's clinch hold.

1. **From the clinch hold position, place your palms under your opponent's elbows.**

2. **Lift your opponent's elbow up as you duck under.**

   Continue to push the elbow over your head.

3. **Keep your head tight to the back of the shoulder and grab the waist.**

Chapter 6

The Takedown: Getting to the Ground

*A*lthough the stand-up game may be exciting for the MMA spectator, the more surefire way to make a submission on your opponent is to take him to the ground. Because most fighters don't go to the ground on their own, you must employ a *takedown,* the move designed to off-balance an opponent and bring him to the ground. It involves preparation, evaluation, and some basic physics. You can take your opponent down in several different ways. In this chapter, I walk you through the double leg takedown, the single leg takedown, and the hip toss. I also show you how to defend against being taken down yourself.

Establishing a Solid Wrestling Stance

Before you can even think about executing an effective takedown, you need to establish a proper wrestling stance. Finding your wrestling stance allows you to both defend against an opponent's attack and initiate your own offensive moves. From your wrestling stance, you can evaluate how to enter your takedown with an efficient technique and then change your level so that your center of gravity is lower than your opponent's in order to obtain the most amount of power.

A good wrestling stance is both offensive and defensive. A fighter in this position can rapidly respond to his opponent's attack with a defense or an attack of his own. Perfecting your wrestling stance provides you with a strong base in any competition. The following six actions are essential to an effective wrestling stance:

   ✔ **Bend your knees.** Bent knees are vital in the fighting game. A fighter with bent legs is prepared for anything, and much like a coiled spring, he can explode with power in an instant.

   ✔ **Keep your elbows in.** Your palms should be facing in and protecting your head. Bend your elbows slightly toward each other to protect your inside.

   ✔ **Feel power in your feet.** Your feet should be no more than shoulder-width apart — never crossed. Try to feel your weight evenly distributed throughout your feet.

✓ **Keep your back straight.** A strong core is your greatest strength and is essential for a successful wrestling stance. An aligned spine keeps your center strong for any upcoming offensive and defensive moves.

✓ **Use small steps.** Unless you're attacking, taking small steps ensures you'll maintain a strong wrestling stance. Taking large steps weakens your stance because with each step you must find a new center. Small steps, on the other hand, allow you to maintain the same center.

✓ **Stay compact and keep low.** Keep your center of gravity lower than that of your opponent's. A low stance allows you to bring the most power possible into a movement like a takedown.

 If you want to attack from your wrestling stance, you must change your level. To be able to move your opponent, your center of gravity must be lower than his center of gravity. Much like how you've been taught to pick up heavy objects, you must drop low and draw strength and power from your lower body. If you train and use the drills listed in Chapter 13, getting into a takedown position will become part of your body's natural flow.

Trying Out the Double Leg Takedown

As its name implies, a *double leg takedown* involves taking an opponent to the mat by wrapping up both of his legs. You may attempt a takedown at any time during a bout, provided you remember to strike before you commit for a takedown so as not to expose your move.

 A good time to go for a double leg takedown is when you want to drop away from danger. If your opponent makes a forward movement with a strike, drop to your wrestling stance.

To perform a double leg takedown, do the following:

1. **Assume the standard stand-up fighting stance.**

   For tips on getting into this stance, flip to Chapter 4.

2. **Change levels and get into your wrestling stance.**

   Changing your level means lowering your center of gravity. Do so just like how you'd prepare for some heavy lifting — by bending your knees and keeping your back straight.

3. **From your wrestling stance, drop into the runner's stance position with your back straight and your back foot on your toes.**

   The *runner's stance* is a position of great strength and explosive power. This power comes from the body's alignment, so keep your head up and your back straight. Because you want to strike your opponent with your forehead, avoid turning your head away or down; doing the opposite affects your impact because your body isn't lined up for power.

4. **From the runner's stance, with your head up and back straight, run through your opponent's body by striking the center of his torso with your shoulder, while simultaneously pulling his legs out from under him.**

   Pulling your opponent's legs out from under him is a technique that's more commonly referred to as *pulling out the bottom.*

5. **Use your momentum to drive through your opponent and pull his legs out to bring him down.**

6. **Immediately move into a dominant position if you want to fight on the ground.**

   The mount is a good dominant position to use; see Chapter 8 for more information. In this case, I'm going for a side mount.

A More Advanced Technique: The Single Leg Takedown

During a competition, the single leg takedown is a riskier takedown option than the double leg approach described in the preceding section. Why? Because you're more prone to injury or counters. For an inexperienced fighter, moving in for a single leg takedown puts you in the vulnerable position of having your head near your opponent's knee. This technique only takes away one of your opponent's legs; therefore, your opponent may still have a base with his other leg to be able to counter your attack. When the double leg takedown isn't available, like when your opponent is in midkick, then you can attempt a single leg takedown.

The target of this takedown is the front leg, as opposed to the center of your opponent's body in the double leg takedown. Here's how to do it:

1. **Assume the standard stand-up fighting stance.**

   Throw some punches to keep your opponent in stand-up fighting mode.

2. **Change levels and get into your wrestling stance.**

   Just like how you'd get ready to lift a heavy object, lower your center of gravity by bending your knees and keeping your back straight.

3. **Crouch down and swing your rear leg to the side of your opponent's front leg; grab hold of his front leg and pull it into your body.**

   Ideally, your opponent's front leg should be between your legs after the first part of this step. This is the position before impact — the single leg takedown position. Notice the way my legs are positioned around my opponent's leg, with one crouched for power and the other posted out for leverage.

4. **Position your head on the inside of your opponent's thigh and your shoulder above his knee. Use your back leg to power forward in the crouch position so you can use your shoulder to strike your opponent. Drive in with your shoulder as you pull his leg out.**

   Your head should be tight against the outside of your opponent's thigh with your shoulder above his knee.

5. **As you crouch to get his front leg and swing your rear leg out, you should automatically be in position with your head and shoulder tight around his leg, pushing him forward while pulling his leg out.**

6. **Immediately climb on top for the superior grappling position.**

   Here, I've got side control and a chance to apply an arm bar.

Striking to a Takedown

If you shoot directly into a takedown, the odds are good your opponent will recognize your plan and defend against it. Striking your opponent, however, causes him to react and potentially open himself up for a successful takedown. Here's how to use a jab to cover your takedown:

1. **Start out in your normal fighting stance.**

   You want to make it look like you want to continue to stand up and fight.

2. **Jab your opponent. Immediately change levels and get into your wrestling stance.**

   See Chapter 4 for guidance on forming an effective jab.

   To change levels, simply lower your center of gravity so that it's below your opponent's.

3. **Continue with a single leg or double leg takedown.**

   See the previous sections in this chapter for descriptions of these takedown moves.

Perfecting the Hip Toss

The *hip toss,* a common judo throw, is when you pull your opponent's hips over your own and use your hips to move him where you want him to go.

1. **Grip your opponent's arm with one hand and grasp around the shoulder with your other arm.**

   A tight grip ensures a strong follow-through.

2. **Bring your hips all the way in so that they're parallel with your opponent's hips.**

3. **Bend your knee to get below your opponent's hips. Pop your hips back and use that momentum to pull your opponent over your body.**

You have to be quick to take your opponent off guard.

4. **When your opponent is on the ground, move into a dominant grappling position or begin striking.**

In this case, I have the opportunity to throw some punches to the head.

Defending against a Takedown

You can avoid takedowns in several ways. Here, I present two:

Never let your opponent get inside and control your center. For example, letting your opponent's leg be between your legs, with his arms clinched around your inside, is a bad position. Swimming your arms in front of you is key to redirecting control. If you find that your opponent's leg is splitting your center, pop your hips out and away.

Use the sprawl to defend against the double or single leg takedown. The *sprawl* is your most important defensive move against either of these takedowns. In this move, you shoot your legs out and dig your hips toward the ground while pressing them on your opponent's head to control his movement. This positioning leaves your opponent facedown with the bulk of your weight on his shoulders, neck, and head. A vulnerable position for your opponent, the sprawl leaves him available to any number of attacks.

The takedown is an important move because of its effect on a fight. Usually if you take down your opponent, you'll land in a dominant position with your opponent on his back. Being on your back, however, doesn't mean defeat, because you can still fight from the guard position (described in Chapter 7).

Part III
Grappling: You Gotta Have a Ground Game

In this part . . .

The chapters in this part are designed to get you comfortable with many forms of close-quarters ground fighting, also known as grappling. I show you effective techniques whether you're lying on the mat, fighting on top of your opponent, or trying to escape your opponent's grasp.

Chapter 7

Working from the Guard

In This Chapter

▶ Perfecting the versatile guard position

▶ Making sure you can attack from any version of the guard

▶ Working on your submission holds and escape moves

*F*ew positions in MMA allow you to both defend yourself and attack your opponent with great fluidity — the guard is one of them. The guard is a basic and essential position in the ground-fighting game. It's also the simplest and easiest defensive position you can attack from. In this chapter, I show you all things guard-related, including the core position of the guard, submission holds from the guard, and the various strikes and escapes you can make within this versatile position.

Practicing the Core Position: Passive Guard

If you've been taken to the ground and your opponent is on top of you, the guard is the best position you can employ. Why? Because the guard is meant to protect you by keeping your opponent close so he has little space to wind up and strike you. When forming the core of the guard position, *passive guard,* you want to do the following:

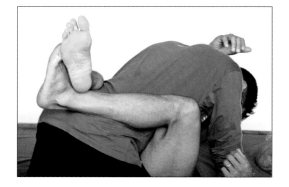

Lock your legs behind your opponent's back. While lying on your back, wrap your legs around your opponent's body and lock them together at the ankles. Eliminate any extra distance between you and your opponent by squeezing your legs tight around his lower ribs and waist.

Grab the back of your opponent's head and hold it down while holding his tricep with your other hand. Your front hand should be placed on the back of your opponent's head. Hook your dominant hand on his tricep.

Round your back. Because you're controlling your opponent's head and arm, you need to keep your back rounded and ready for any offensive or defensive moves he may try to spring on you. Remember to remain active by throwing strikes and looking for submission opportunities; doing so makes your guard position more effective. (Later in this chapter, I show you some of the specific strikes and submission holds you can do from the guard.)

The following positions are ones that you flow through from the passive guard in order to accomplish another technique.

Half guard

The half guard is a defensive position and is usually used in conjunction with a submission attempt. Instead of hooking your legs behind your opponent's back like in the passive guard, you hook both of your legs to hold one of your opponent's legs.

Active guard

The *active guard* is the same position as the passive guard, except that your legs aren't locked. (I call this position the "active" guard to remind my students to fight actively and aggressively when in it.) *Note:* This position allows your opponent the opportunity to escape, so you should only use it briefly when trying to apply another technique such as a sweep or a submission.

When in active guard, you should always finish a technique as quickly as possible so as not to exert a lot of energy. Here's how to form the position:

1. **Grab the back of your opponent's head with your front hand.**

2. **Grasp your opponent's arm at the tricep with your dominant hand.**

   Because you're giving up more control by opening your legs, you need to maintain some level of control by holding on to your opponent's head and arm.

Guard sit-up

The guard sit-up position is a way to create energy before you move on to a submission or a sweep.

1. **Really work the guard to keep your opponent from suspecting you might be preparing to change positions.**

2. **Let go of your opponent's head with your dominant hand.**

3. **Use your front arm to hook over your opponent's left shoulder and sit up.**

   You create strength by forming angles with your limbs, so make sure your arms and legs achieve 90-degree angles. Also, keep your chest up and spine straight and pinch your opponent's shoulder for control.

Guard posture

If you're in your opponent's guard (meaning you're in the top position and not on your back), you can flow into guard posture to prevent the execution of most techniques your opponent will attempt.

1. **Scoot your body as close as possible to your opponent's while straightening your back and sitting over your heels on the balls of your feet.**

2. **Press your opponent's hips down and keep your back and arms straight, elbows in, and chin up.**

   Don't allow your back to bend or be pulled over. Your weight should be centered between your knees and your feet.

Striking from Passive Guard

Although the passive guard is a defensive position, you can go on the offensive from it by striking your opponent using any of the moves described in the following sections.

Punch to head

Punching your opponent's head is another way to inflict damage and get your opponent to react or release the position.

1. **From the passive guard, release your dominant hand from holding your opponent's tricep.**

2. **Punch your opponent's head.**

    Repeat as necessary. If you don't already
    know, the ears really hurt when punched.

3. **Return to grasping your opponent's tricep.**

    Punching your opponent's body is a great way to inflict damage while setting him up
    for a potential submission because he may expose another area of his body while
    trying to block your strike. So if your opponent gives you the opportunity to do so,
    punch to the body as well as the head.

Heel kick

A heel kick can be devastating to your opponent. Continual kicks to one area can cause
a lot of pain, and your opponent may react in a way that opens him up for a submission
maneuver.

1. **From the passive guard, keep your legs
   tightly wrapped around your opponent's
   body and maintain a firm grip on his
   head.**

2. **Unlock your legs, keeping one of them tight against your opponent's body.**

3. **With your other leg, use your heel to strike your opponent's back or side.**

   A well-placed kick with your heel can really do some damage. But you may not have the range of movement to strike with power. In those cases, repeated kicks can still wear down your opponent. Strike the low back, kidney area, and hips.

4. **After striking, lock your legs back into the passive guard position.**

Attacking from Inside an Opponent's Passive Guard

When inside an opponent's passive guard, you can implement either of the offensive moves described in the next two sections.

Guard head punch

Strikes from inside your opponent's guard can be effective, but you must be quick and remember to protect yourself. This move can be used separately or as part of a combination. Either way, you must start in the core position of passive guard, so be sure to check out that section in this chapter before moving forward.

1. **From guard posture inside your opponent's passive guard, jab his head.**

   Be quick and make sure your arms are safe from submissions. If you need pointers on throwing a jab, turn to Chapter 4.

2. **Return to guard posture.**

   Protect your head and keep your arms out of his grasp.

Guard body elbow

Because being in your opponent's passive guard keeps you close to him, an elbow to his body can be both an easy and effective tactic.

1. **From guard posture inside your opponent's passive guard, elbow his body.**

   Be quick. Your opponent is going to try to pull your head in close if you lean into your elbow blows for too long. And be sure to cover your face with your opposite hand.

2. **Return to guard posture.**

   Be ready to throw more punches and elbows.

Parrying, Blocking, and Catching in Passive Guard

If you're in the passive guard when your opponent attempts a strike, your best bet is to either parry and block or simply catch his punch.

Parrying is the act of moving your upper body aside as you block an incoming punch. Here's how to do it:

1. **When a punch comes, use your hands like windshield wipers to slap that punch away.**

2. **Move your upper body and head out of the way.**

   Just like a catcher in baseball, you can catch a punch with your hands instead of getting hit in the face. If you're able to catch your opponent's punch, you may be able to move to an arm bar or another submission hold.

Applying Submission Holds

The following sections illustrate submission holds you can execute when you have your opponent in your active guard position (see the related section earlier in this chapter for guidance on forming the active guard).

Turning arm bar

The turning arm bar is best attempted when your opponent extends his arm toward your chest. Sometimes fighters leave their arms open when blocking or reacting to a strike, so look for these golden opportunities and do the following:

1. **From the active guard position, grab your opponent's wrist and hold it tight to your chest.**

2. **With your palm up, hook your other hand behind your opponent's knee and pull yourself sideways.**

3. **As you turn, throw one leg over your opponent's head and move your whole body sideways.**

   Exhale to build energy for this move.

4. **Lift your hips, raising your body up so only your head and shoulder are on the ground.**

   Be sure to keep your back straight. Your opponent's elbow should be at your groin.

5. **Pull your opponent's arm down and drive your hips into the back of the elbow to execute the submission.**

   Think of pulling your feet together, as well as your knees, and bringing your heels to your butt for perfect execution.

Guard sit-up front choke

This combination move starts with a guard sit-up and finishes with a front choke.

1. **Perform a guard sit-up to your opponent's shoulder.**

   See the "Guard sit-up" section earlier in this chapter to figure out how to get into this starting position.

2. **Switch your grip from over the shoulder to around your opponent's neck.**

   Scoot your butt out to make space for this grip.

Here's a look at this move from the opposite side.

3. **Grab your other wrist and maintain your grip as you return to the closed guard position.**

4. **Roll your shoulder back to finish the submission.**

Guard sit-up shoulder lock

You can easily flow into the shoulder lock from the guard sit-up position by following these instructions:

1. **Perform a guard sit-up to your opponent's shoulder.**

   You should have your opponent's arm hooked underneath your armpit.

2. **Pull the shoulder to the mat and lie back down on the mat with your legs locked.**

3. **With your free hand, grab your opponent's wrist; then grab your own arm with your other arm and create a figure four.**

   Your body, head, and figure four submission grip should be 45 degrees away from your opponent.

4. **Lift your fists toward your opponent's head, putting pressure on the shoulder to finish the submission.**

Here's a close-up of this submission hold.

Escaping from the Guard

When grappling, the best position to be in is a dominant one such as the mount (or any of the other dominant positions described in Chapter 8). But in order to obtain such a dominant position, you first need to free yourself from your opponent's guard.

Following are some easy techniques for escaping from the guard.

Sweep

The guard sweep flips you over to the mount, a top position. From the mount, you can either strike your opponent or attempt submissions. (See Chapter 9 for a specific submission you can attempt from the mount.)

1. **From the passive guard, grab control of your opponent's wrists.**

   Be forewarned: This maneuver is easier said than done.

2. **Keep your elbows in and raise his wrists above your head. Roll him forward.**

   This move takes some strength, so put some energy into it.

3. **Pull your hips out and bring your knee and shin across your opponent's belly, with your foot hooking against his hip bone.**

   Being able to move your legs and hips quickly while in the guard takes a lot of practice, but if you can develop active hips and legs when on the ground, your opponents are going to have a hard time controlling the action.

4. **With your other leg at the base of your opponent's legs, pull his arms overhead as you sweep your legs through his.**

   You're hoping this move takes your opponent by surprise.

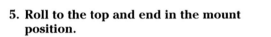

5. **Roll to the top and end in the mount position.**

   Now you're on top and better able to dictate the flow of the fight.

Kick over

Use the kick over when you attempt a turning arm bar by extending your hips but can't for some reason complete the submission hold or your opponent blocks you by pressing down.

1. **From the extended hips position of the turning arm bar, pull your hips down.**

   Here, I'm bringing his arm closer to my body for better leverage.

2. **Reach in to your opponent's closest knee.**

   Notice I'm going for my sparring partner's knee with my right hand.

3. **Pull his knee across your face and kick your hips out at a 45-degree angle.**

I've just about got him rolled over.

4. **Obtain a dominant position.**

   Personally, I prefer using the mount position described in Chapter 8. If the mount isn't for you, Chapter 8 features seven other dominant positions you can try.

Chapter 8

Flowing through the Eight Positions of Power

In This Chapter

▶ Grasping the foundation of submission wrestling

▶ Perfecting the eight dominant positions

*T*his chapter brings you to the foundation of Shamrock MMA: submission wrestling. A strong attack in submission fighting comes from a foundation of balance and control. Think of your weight as your first weapon. If you apply your weight while in a correct position, you can completely control your opponent while leaving your limbs free to attack. Balance and control is achieved when all of your weight is focused on your opponent and none of your weight is on the mat.

What follows in this chapter are the eight dominant positions in submission wrestling. The positions are numbered because they flow from one to another. After reviewing all the positions, work with a partner and practice going through each one in a continuous flow. This exercise builds your muscle memory for the positions and fosters the balance and control you need for attacks.

Position 1: Head and Arm Hold

Position 1 begins with your opponent on his back. Sit next to his head and arm, scooting as close to his body as you possibly can. Following is how the finished position should look:

✔ Your bottom leg is at 90 degrees, your top leg is at 90 degrees, and you're on the ball of your foot.

✔ Your hips are close to your opponent's armpit.

When in this position, be sure to

✔ Cup the back of your opponent's head, pull his chin to his chest, and control his tricep by pulling his elbow into your body.

✔ Stay centered. Avoid leaning forward or backward.

Position 2: Side Mount

The side mount begins with your opponent lying flat on his back and you lying sideways across his body. Here's what to do next:

1. **Test your balance by lifting all of your limbs off the mat.**

   Pretend you're a superhero flying through the sky.

2. **Control your opponent by evenly balancing your weight like a blanket over his body.**

3. **To hold the position, find angles with your arms and legs that don't release your body weight.**

   Your elbows should be at 90 degrees with your opponent's arm in between both of your arms. Your knees should be on the mat, and you should be on the balls of your feet. The more flexible you are, the tighter your position.

Position 3: Head Wrestle

Position 3 begins with your opponent flat on his back. A well-executed version of the head wrestle looks like this:

- ✔ **Your hip bone is on your opponent's temple.** You can use your hip bone to move or distract, as well as to attack your opponent's face, temple, or ear.
- ✔ **Your elbows are in your opponent's armpits at a 90-degree angle, and your hands are gripping his hips.** This control allows you to feel your opponent's movements.
- ✔ **Your knees are on the mat, and you're on the balls of your feet.**

When in Position 3, use your weight as a weapon. You can gain the upper-hand on your opponent by becoming dead weight on him.

Position 4: The Mount

Position 4 starts with your opponent flat on his back. Form this position by doing the following:

1. **Match your hips with your opponent's hips.**

   Your arms and legs should be to the side of your opponent's body.

2. **Test your balance by lifting all of your limbs off the mat, like you're Superman.**

3. **Control your opponent by evenly balancing your weight over his body, like a human blanket.**

   Focus all of your weight on your opponent's body and test for proper positioning by lifting all of your limbs up and then resting them again.

Your head should be down near the bottom of your opponent's head. Additionally, your elbows and knees should be at 90 degrees with your elbows above your opponent's shoulders. At this time, your knees are down on the mat, and you're on the balls of your feet so that you can react quickly.

Position 5: Leg Hold

To perform a leg hold, slide through the guard from Position 4 and scoop up both of your opponent's legs. Then proceed with these steps:

1. **With one knee down, bring your other knee up for balance as you lift your chin and chest.**

2. **Wrap your forearms around your opponent's legs at his Achilles tendon.**

   The *Achilles tendon* is the area behind your ankle on the back of your leg, between your heel and your calf muscle. The lower the better.

3. **Place your fists together, knuckle to knuckle, with your thumbs up to your chin.**

   Be sure not to clasp your hands together because doing so weakens your position.

4. **Plant your front leg and lift your hips forward to control your opponent's legs.**

Position 6: Rear Mount

Position 6 is the rear mount. To flow into this position from the leg hold, turn your opponent over using the control you have over his legs. When your opponent is flat on his stomach, proceed with the following:

1. Match your hips with your opponent's hips, making sure your arms and legs are to the side of his body.

2. Lift all of your limbs off the mat in order to test your balance.

3. Control your opponent by evenly balancing your weight like a blanket over his body.

   Focus all of your weight on your opponent's body and test for proper positioning by lifting all of your limbs up and then bringing them back down. Think of yourself blanketing your opponent.

4. At this point, your head is down near the back of your opponent's head.

   Your knees are at 90 degrees, and your elbows (also at 90 degrees) are above your opponent's shoulders. Stay on the balls of your feet.

Position 7: Rear Side Mount

Position 7, the rear side mount, is like the rear mount but with side control. Here's how to do it:

1. **Mount your opponent from the rear side and focus your weight on him.**

2. **Reach across your opponent's face with your near hand and hook his shoulder to secure control.**

   The best place to hook for control is the *anterior deltoid* (the outside of the shoulder).

   Make sure both of your elbows are at 90 degrees with your other arm across your opponent's hip bone. Your knees should be down, and you should be on the balls of your feet. Keep your weight on the body.

Position 8: Rear Head Wrestle

Position 8 is the rear head wrestle. Similar to Position 3, it begins with you taking your opponent's head for control.

1. **Push your rib cage out and set it on your opponent's head.**

   At this point, your opponent's head is in your stomach or rib cage.

   Use your weight and rib cage to hold him down.

2. **Keep your elbows hooked in your opponent's armpits at a 90-degree angle.**

   Your hands should be on your opponent's hips, your knees should be on the mat, and you should be positioned on the balls of your feet.

3. **Hold both hips with your hands to feel for movement. Focus your dead weight on your opponent's body.**

   In doing so, you can successfully maintain control over him.

Chapter 9

Submitting to No One: Using the Right Submission Techniques

In This Chapter

▶ Incorporating submission grips into your repertoire

▶ Flowing into submission holds from the eight dominant positions

I n Chapter 8, I cover the eight dominant positions. Each position in that chapter has an associated submission hold that you can apply on an opponent. I present these submission holds as well as several submission grips in this chapter. ***Note:*** You can only safely put these moves into practice if you've mastered the dominant positions.

Submission Grips

Every submission technique is designed to inflict the most damage with the least amount of physical effort. Three submission grips are used in most submission holds. Perfecting these grips prevents you from exerting excess physical effort.

Long grip

The *long grip* is a skeletal hold that allows you to hang on for the longest time. It requires little energy but has strength for extended periods of time. Use the long grip as a defensive hold to keep your opponent down if you're mounted and can't get up, or if you're in a clinch. Because this grip uses the skeletal muscles, it's not as strong as grips that use larger muscles. Here's how to do this move:

1. **Turn your hands in opposite directions and hook your fingers together.**

2. **Keep your thumbs pointing in different directions with your elbows straight out.**

3. **Relax your arms.**

Strong grip

The *strong grip* is exactly what it says it is — a strong grip! It's the strongest grip, used for explosive movements and holds like the Achilles hold and the center choke. The only con is that it's an inflexible grip that you can only use for a short amount of time. Here's how you make a strong grip:

1. **Place your hands palm to palm.**

2. **Move your forefinger away from your middle finger and place the thumb of your other hand in this newly created space.**

   It doesn't matter which hand is which in this grip.

3. **Clasp your palms together and hold to keep the lock.**

4. **Use all the muscles in your upper body for a strong grip.**

Figure four

A *figure four* grip is when you hook one of your limbs (legs or arms) in the crook of the other, or when you grab your own wrist while your other hand is holding one of your opponent's limbs. It's very strong and used in many submission holds like the arm bar and the telephone lock. However, this grip is hard to set up because you must either move or trick your opponent into the position.

How you perform a figure four depends on how you want to use it. In the photos throughout this chapter, you see that you can form the figure four grip with your legs for a leg submission or with your hand and wrist for an arm submission.

Applying Submission Holds from the Eight Positions of Power

The purpose of a submission hold is to apply pain or pressure to a specific body part so that your opponent gives up and taps out, which is basically the same as saying "Uncle!" Some submissions are choke holds, which, if successfully applied, will cause your opponent to pass out if he doesn't tap.

A properly trained opponent knows when to tap. You can't ease up on your submission holds out of pity. If you have your opponent locked in a hold and he can't escape, either he'll tap or the referee will stop the fight. Keep applying pressure until either occurs. Don't forget that your job in the ring is to keep working until the fight is over.

Position 1: Head and arm hold submission options

From Position 1, the head and arm hold, you can apply either the shoulder lock or the straight arm bar.

Shoulder lock

Try the shoulder lock when your opponent pushes his face and body away in an attempt to create space between you and him. The shoulder lock attacks the tendons that hold the shoulder in its socket. When you apply the shoulder lock effectively, your opponent will feel like his tendons are tearing.

1. **From Position 1, grab hold of your opponent's forearm.**

2. **Press your opponent's arm into the crook of your bottom leg and hook the arm in between your thigh and calf for control.**

3. **Use your upper leg to cross your ankles and pull your bottom leg back into a figure four position.**

   Doing so secures your opponent's arm in the submission hold.

4. **Pull your opponent's chin to your chest and press your hips through his shoulder to finish the hold.**

   Listen or wait for a tap out.

Straight arm bar

If the shoulder lock submission doesn't work, you can flow into the next submission — the straight arm bar. The straight arm bar is a popular submission that's attempted pretty often. In fact, it's the go-to submission when you see an opponent's open arm. If you do it right, your opponent will tap because he'll feel like his arm might break.

1. **When your opponent's arm is straightened to block the shoulder lock or attempt an escape, make sure you have a firm grip on his wrist.**

2. **Place your top leg on the extended arm and use the weight of your leg as a weapon.**

3. **Lift your bottom leg and press the top leg down to create a leveraging motion in order to maximize the hold.**

Position 2: Side mount submission options

In Position 2, the side mount, you're looking directly at your opponent's arm, making it a prime target for submissions. You can attempt the telephone lock or the straight arm bar.

Telephone lock

When you're in Position 2, the telephone lock applies pressure to your opponent's shoulder.

1. **When your opponent's hand is near his head, place some weight on his wrist.**

   The amount of pressure you place on his wrist depends on his flexibility; simply apply pressure until he taps.

   Maintain an even distribution of your body weight over your opponent's body.

2. **Reach your other hand under your opponent's elbow and grasp your own wrist, forming the figure four grip.**

   Keep the hand pressed into the mat.

3. **Set your weight fully on your opponent's body by rolling your weight straight across his body and away from the hold.**

4. **Lift your shoulder and roll your wrists to finish the hold.**

   Your opponent's elbow should rise as you push his wrist down. Don't turn your body or move your position in any way. Instead, use your weight to move your opponent's elbow on top of his body, with the elbow pointed toward the sky.

Straight arm bar

If the telephone lock submission hold isn't successful, you can flow into the next submission — the straight arm bar.

1. **Place weight on your opponent's wrist to control his arm.**

   You really want to press his arm into the mat.

2. **Release the weight and reposition the wrist straight and slightly above the shoulder height of your opponent.**

3. **Swim your hand behind your opponent's shoulder and under his elbow to create leverage.**

4. **Finish with one elbow on the mat and your hand grasping your own wrist, creating a figure four grip and applying pressure to your opponent's wrist to force it toward the mat.**

   Make sure your opponent's thumb is pointed up to the ceiling. When his thumb is up, his elbow is down, leaving you in the most effective area for attack.

Position 3: Pec choke

From the head wrestle position, also known as Position 3, you can apply the pec choke.

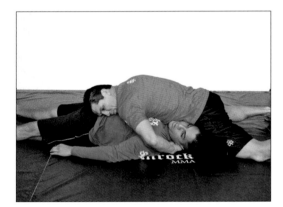

1. **Reach your hand behind your opponent's head on the side where he's facing away so you can catch his chin in your chest.**

   Doing so sets up the hold so that he can't escape, allowing you to attack his throat.

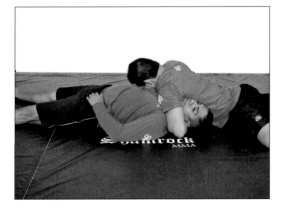

2. **Slide your hand through as you push yourself down and catch your opponent's chin in your chest area.**

   Be sure to catch the chin so as to expose your opponent's neck.

3. **With your other arm, catch your opponent's arm and raise it above his head. When his arm is above shoulder height, reach around it and grab your own wrist.**

4. **To set the hold, push your shoulder onto your opponent's exposed neck and focus your body weight to that shoulder.**

Don't squeeze your arm to finish. Instead, tighten and focus your weight by elevating your body slightly.

Because this hold attacks the windpipe, it's more of a strangle than a choke.

Position 4: Mount choke

Position 4 is the mount position, and fittingly enough, from it you can attempt the mount choke, which targets your opponent's throat.

1. **Take your weight from the center and move it to one side.**

2. Reach your closest hand to your opponent's body and hook his shoulder. Hold the shoulder down as your forearm and elbow cross your opponent's neck.

3. Be sure not to move your weight back to the center.

Doing so weakens the side applying the choke.

Position 5: Leg hold submission options

Position 5, the leg hold, has you focusing on your opponent's legs, so it makes perfect sense to attack them with the Achilles hold or the toe hold.

Achilles hold

Here's a no-brainer: The Achilles hold puts pressure on your opponent's Achilles tendon. Simple as that.

1. Keep your opponent's legs locked in your arms.

2. Drop the leg of your opponent that's closest to your downed knee.

3. Sit to your side and wrap both of your legs around your opponent's leg.

Use your other hand to support yourself as you fall backward.

4. Slide your wrist under your opponent's Achilles tendon and maintain a 90-degree angle.

The *Achilles tendon* is the area behind your ankle on the back of your leg between your heel and your calf muscle.

5. **With your thumb facing up, use your wrist bone as a weapon and squeeze your knees together while focusing energy through your hips.**

   Don't let the angle of your arm change, or else your hold will weaken.

6. **Drive your hips into the Achilles and maintain the position.**

Toe hold

If you don't have any luck with the Achilles hold, you can flow into the next submission — the toe hold.

1. **Slide your wrist out from under your opponent's ankle but use your elbow to keep his leg pressed to your body.**

2. **Roll your shoulders flat to the mat and grab the entire width of your opponent's foot (above the last knuckles).**

3. **Squeeze the knuckles together and lock your tricep straight. Hold this position and push energy through your hips.**

4. **Extend your body backward to finish the hold. Keep your knees tight.**

   Don't allow your arm to bend and make sure to use only your hips for attack.

Position 6: Rear choke

Position 6, the rear mount, gives you the opportunity to apply the rear choke. A popular submission, the rear choke is sure to make your opponent tap when applied correctly.

1. **Wrap one arm around your opponent's chin and grasp your opposite bicep to create a figure-four lock.**

   It's important to work your arm under his chin.

2. Use your opposite arm to push off the back of your opponent's head.

3. Press your head down against the arm that's under your opponent's chin.

4. Pull this arm under your opponent's neck back in a scissor motion against his neck.

Wait for your opponent to tap out.

Position 7: Neck Crank

From the rear side mount (Position 7), you can attempt a submission with the neck crank because your opponent's head and neck are what's closest to you.

1. **Switch your hips toward your opponent's head while maintaining the crossface hold.**

   A *crossface* is a sawing motion across your opponent's face beginning at your wrist and ending at your elbow or forearm.

2. **When your hips are almost switched, grab your other arm at the bicep with your crossface arm.**

3. **Keep weight on your opponent's body and sit back to finish the hold until he taps.**

Here's the hold viewed from the opposite side.

Remember: The neck crank is fairly dangerous, so practice it with caution at all times. Listen to your partner.

Position 8: Front choke

If you're in Position 8, the rear head wrestle, you can apply the front choke because you're already pushing your rib cage out on top of your opponent's head. Going for a front choke is just a few steps away:

1. **Reach your two hands under your opponent's body and clasp them together palm to palm.**

2. **Gently slide your clasped hands under your opponent's chin and keep your rib cage thrust out.**

3. Pull your elbows to your side and keep your rib cage out for the choke.

4. To maximize the front choke, get to your feet and use your hips to roll under the choke.

5. Be sure to keep your rib cage on top of your opponent's head with your elbows back and tighten your grip until he submits.

Chapter 10

Great Escapes

Sometimes you're going to find yourself on the wrong side of the eight dominant positions, and you're going to need a way to escape. In this chapter, I present escape options for each position. (The basic technique of these escapes is built from mat drills, which you can read all about in Chapter 13.) I believe you can escape most submissions by changing your position and going with the energy of the hold. This idea comes from the theory of constant movement, a tool for advanced grapplers and strikers alike.

The goal of constant movement is to create energy and confusion. All movement is followed by either a reaction to the movement or a counter to the movement. Think of the position escapes in this chapter as new beginnings for aggressive offensive moves and submission holds.

Position 1 (Head and Arm Hold) Escapes

You have three escape options when stuck in your opponent's Position 1 (the head and arm hold); all three start by attacking his body positioning. *Note:* When on the defensive end of Position 1, most of your strength is going to come from the 90-degree angles of your lower body.

Bending backward: The bridge

The bridge is the most powerful escape; it also requires the most amount of muscle exertion. Although the bridge is easy to perform, it's hard on your body. You have to focus a lot of power through your hips. Always be aware when doing this move and don't attempt to pull your opponent across your shoulders without the hip lift described in the following steps.

1. **Wrap your arms around your opponent's body and clasp your hands with a strong grip.**

   Keep your hands close to you.

2. **Walk your hips under your opponent's body.**

   Quick hips can really help you here as well as a strong neck and lower back.

3. **Raise your hips to the ceiling and arch your back as you roll up to your head and shoulder.**

   Your hips do the lifting and your arms keep your opponent in position.

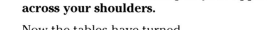

4. Look toward the mat and pull your opponent across your shoulders.

Now the tables have turned.

Practice makes for perfection (and safety!) when it comes to the bridge, so check out the bridge drill I provide in Chapter 13.

Enclosing your opponent: Leg wrap

If your opponent tucks his head or moves away, you can perform the leg wrap.

1. Continue to move your hips under your opponent. While maintaining a strong grip around your opponent's body, wrap your upper leg around the inside of his closest leg.

2. **Throw your leg over and form a figure four with your other leg.**

   Flip to Chapter 9 for more on the figure four.

3. **Maintain your grip as you work to move your head out from under your opponent's arm.**

4. **Use a strong grip and leg lock to pull open your opponent's body and slide your head out so that you're on his back.**

Saving face: Head hook roll

A more advanced technique, the head hook roll can be a very effective escape from your opponent's Position 1.

1. **Walk away from your opponent's hips to set up the escape.**

   Push away with your legs and hips. Your opponent expects you to go under his hips.

2. **Place your close hand on your opponent's face and push his head up.**

3. **Roll your lower body up to hook your leg over his face.**

   He's not going to like this turn of events.

4. Pull your opponent's head down with your leg as you roll your body up to finish the escape.

Position 2 (Side Mount) Escapes

When your opponent has you in his Position 2 (the side mount), you have a couple escape options.

Going out the side door

For maximum control, apply this escape (known as "out the side door") toward your opponent's head or feet.

1. Begin by sliding both of your hands under your opponent's body so that they're near your hips.

2. **Turn your body to the side slightly and dig your heels into the mat.**

   Quickness makes all the difference here.

3. **Pulling with your heels and arms, slide your body out the side.**

Making like a shrimp

In order to shift from under your opponent's Position 2 to the guard (described in Chapter 7), use the shrimp. Granted, it's not technically a true escape because you don't achieve a top position, but you do put yourself in a better position by moving to the guard. You can employ the shrimp to not only change your position but also to set up another escape attempt.

1. **Pull your heels to your butt before pushing off of them and shooting your hips out and back.**

   This move creates space between you and your opponent.

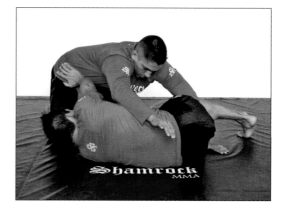

2. **Slide your legs in, making sure one is behind your opponent's back and the other is across his belly.**

3. Extend the hip of your trapped leg and place that foot on the ground.

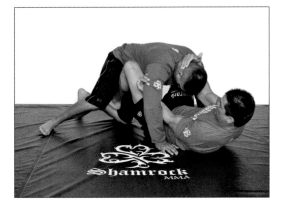

4. Scoot your hips out and cross your legs behind your opponent to achieve the guard position.

5. Now that you are in the guard, use the attacks and defenses covered in Chapter 7.

Position 3 (Head Wrestle) Escapes

Imagine that your opponent has you locked in Position 3 (the head wrestle) and that you need to get out before he can apply a *pec choke* (the submission hold associated with Position 3, which I cover in Chapter 9).

This escape, which combines a head hook with a bridge, is best used from Position 3 because you don't expose yourself to possible submissions your opponent could attempt.

1. **Scoot your hips toward your opponent's head to free them and close the space between the two of you.**

2. **Use your free arm to hook your opponent's head and turn your body so that it's 45 degrees away from him.**

3. **With your opponent's head in the crook of your arm, bridge to finish the technique.**

   See the earlier "Bending backward: The bridge" section for step-by-step direction on forming the bridge.

4. **Now that you have your opponent in a head wrestle, go for a pec choke.**

To further practice fighting from Position 3, use the bridge drill found in Chapter 13.

Position 4 (The Mount) Escapes

Many people consider Position 4 (the mount) a finishing position. However, you *can* attempt a few submission holds from it. You can finish off your opponent, but usually just from strikes unless the positioning changes. To escape Position 4, you need to break down the table of strength that's controlling you. The table has four legs of strength you can attack, and the next two sections show you how to do just that.

Working the bridge

Bridging is the best and most powerful way to escape Position 4. To begin, catch one of your opponent's legs and step your foot over the leg you caught to block his foot. Or you can catch your opponent's hand with one of the following options and bridge with your hips. (Check out the earlier "Bending backward: The bridge" section in this chapter for pointers on forming the bridge.) Think about making his four-legged table a two-legged table.

1. **Keep your opponent's elbow at his side and reach your cupped hand into the crook of his arm.**

2. **Pull that side of his body down.**

   Your head and shoulder should be on the mat.

3. Swing your body up and over your opponent.

Another bridging option begins by pulling your opponent's arm over your head.

1. Keep your opponent's arm on the mat.

2. Slide it up and above your head to sweep your opponent as you bridge.

Note: This technique is best used when your opponent counters the previous bridge attack.

Popping that hip

The hip-pop option for escaping Position 4 works best when you're mounted or side mounted. You can also use the hip-pop technique in combination with other escapes. For instance, you can bridge, hip pop, and bridge again to unsettle your opponent.

1. **Place your hands on your opponent's hips.**

   Do this quickly before he starts throwing punches.

2. Bridge your hips in the air.

See the section "Bending backward: The bridge," earlier in this chapter, for guidance on bridging.

3. Raise your hands 45 degrees above your head and bring your knees to your chest.

4. Bring your elbows to your knees in the turtle position.

To perfect your turtle, one of the five animals of MMA fighting, check out Chapter 11.

Position 5 (Leg Hold) Escape

The only real way to escape from Position 5 (the leg hold) is to perform a leg sweep that keeps your opponent from controlling your legs.

1. **Raise your hips off the mat and use your arms for balance.**

   As you can see, this isn't a good position to be in.

2. **Pull your legs into your body to unbalance your opponent.**

   Use your abs and hip flexors for power.

3. **With your opponent off balance, turn your hips to the left or right to throw him off of you.**

   For help forming the bridge, turn to the "Bending backward: The bridge" section found earlier in this chapter.

Position 6 (Rear Mount) Escape

When your opponent has you in Position 6 (the rear mount), you're at risk of being put in a rear choke (described in Chapter 9). Here's how you can escape:

1. **Raise your body up to a solid wrestling stance.**

   Refer to Chapter 6 for more on this stance.

Notice that I'm off the mat and on the balls of my feet.

2. **Sit your hips out and through with your leg at 90 degrees.**

Here, I'm sliding out the front and getting ready to turn around.

Now I'm looking at my opponent and coming around before he can re-engage.

3. Switch your hips and turn into dog position, facing your opponent.

See Chapter 11 for the basics on the dog position.

Position 7 (Rear Side Mount) Escape

Escapes from Position 7 (the rear side mount) mainly involve returning to the dog position (covered in Chapter 11) and using the dog theory to escape.

When you're in the dog position, you're stronger than the person behind you because of your ability to create powerful 90-degree angles and because you're in a sprinters stance.

Escapes you can use from the dog position include the monkey roll, which I show you in Chapter 11.

Position 8 (Rear Head Wrestle) Escape

If your opponent's applying Position 8 (the rear head wrestle), you can employ the sit out to escape before he tries a front choke. Here's how to do it:

1. **Keep your arms on the mat to protect yourself from a choke.**

2. **Bring your knees to your elbows, or place your knee up and on the ball of your foot, touching your elbow.**

   Look out from underneath your opponent's body and work your head out.

3. **Sit out by getting your head out from under your opponent's body.**

   Not sure how to sit out? Simply raise your body into a solid wrestling stance on the side where your head is out. Throw your other leg through 90 degrees from your head so that both your head and body are on the side of your opponent.

4. **Turn into dog position by looking toward your opponent, collapsing your elbow, and switching your hips to face him.**

   Check out Chapter 11 for a detailed description of the dog position.

Chapter 11

Improving Your Ground Game: The Five Animals of MMA

In This Chapter
▶ Surveying the three core animal positions
▶ Adding animal-minded maneuvers to your bag o' tricks

*H*ere's your chance to start thinking about mixed martial arts (MMA) in a new way — through animals. The turtle, dog, cat, monkey, and snake all hold valuable lessons for an MMA fighter. In this chapter, I show you not only the core positions and maneuvers named for these animals but also the various reversals, escapes, and strikes you can attempt from these animal positions.

A Well-Protected Position: The Turtle

From the turtle position, you can control all of your opponent's body weight. Better yet, if your opponent is standing, the turtle position is a well-protected position to be in because all four of your limbs are available for attack. As an added bonus, if your opponent is taller than you, you can easily throw him off balance this way.

The turtle position is also known as the active guard (which I go into detail about in Chapter 7). I like to talk about the turtle position specifically in order to remind my students to act like a turtle with a rounded back — the human version of a protective shell.

The following sections describe the basics of the turtle position, as well as its related moves.

Reviewing the turtle position

Here are the features of the turtle position, which starts with you lying on your back:

✔ Your back is rounded with your elbows to your knees. The result looks much like a turtle lying on its back, protected by a strong shell. Keep your toes up or feet flexed forward to hook your opponent's legs.

✔ If an opponent is on top of you when you're in this position, his thighs are on your shins and your hands are in his armpits. Relax your legs to allow the weight to settle on your hips.

Escaping from the turtle: Turtle elevator

If your opponent is lying on top of you in the turtle position, the turtle elevator is an easy way to move him.

1. **From the turtle position, lift one side of your body by letting the opposite side fall to the mat.**

2. **Hook your opponent's leg and lift on whichever side of your body is falling to the mat.**

3. **Roll onto your opponent and attempt to mount him.**

Employing the takedown: Turtle sweep

The turtle sweep is a perfect takedown to employ when you're in the turtle position and your opponent is standing, which is a very dangerous situation. (For more on the basics of takedowns, turn to Chapter 6.) The following steps show how you can move from a sweep to a leg hold.

1. **Hook your feet behind your opponent's knees.**

   Keep your arms up to protect your face from strikes. Keep your feet flexed to hook the legs.

2. **Grab your opponent's ankles and pull them toward you as you straighten both of your legs in front of you at a 45-degree angle.**

3. Hold onto the ankles as your opponent falls backward.

4. Tuck one foot to your butt while your opposite foot steps on the mat.

5. Maintain a hold on your opponent's ankles as you use the momentum to bring yourself up.

6. **Bring yourself up onto one knee.**

7. **Straighten up as you maneuver to a leg hold.**

   See Chapter 8 for help forming the leg hold.

8. **Pull your opponent's legs to your sides, using your forearms and biceps to lock his feet.**

   You can also stand up to the fighting stance.

Backing Up Your Strength: The Dog

The dog position, which gets its name because you tend to look just like a dog when you're in it, involves turning your back on your opponent. When you turn your back to someone, you have more choices for positional advance or attack than the person behind you. Your opponent can only attempt a choke or a strike. If he attempts either move, he releases any hold he may have of you, opening up the opportunity for you to escape or attempt a submission.

The dog is a very strong position because of its structure with 90-degree angles (as you can see in the following section). It works best when you're grappling with someone who has a background in wrestling because he'll be more apt to take positions that are the foundation of grappling.

This position is strictly for ground fighting in MMA. Don't use it in self-defense situations when you're facing multiple opponents.

Checking out the dog position

The dog position is an easy one to perform. When well-executed, it should look like this:

- ✔ You're on all fours, just like your favorite pooch.
- ✔ Your knees are on the mat with your legs at a 90-degree angle, and you're on the balls of your feet.
- ✔ Your palms are on the mat, and your arms and back are straight.

Attempting a submission from the dog

When in the dog position, you can attempt a straight arm bar on your opponent and force a submission. Here's how:

1. Make sure you're on the balls of your feet even though you're on your hands and knees and giving your opponent your back.

Be mindful that your opponent may attempt a choke from this position.

2. Move one knee up as you attempt to grab one of your opponent's arms above the elbow.

3. **Grab your opponent's wrist and figure four his arm on the same side as your up knee.**

   See Chapter 9 for more on the figure four grip.

4. **Make sure your forearm is under your opponent's elbow.**

5. **Rise to your feet to apply additional pressure to your opponent's arm, forcing a submission.**

A Study in Versatility: The Cat

The cat position gives you the gift of versatility because it's both offensive and defensive. Break out the cat position when your opponent is standing and you're on the ground.

Examining the cat position

When in the cat position, your two limbs are available to protect and strike while one side of your body is on the mat. Here's what it looks like:

- ✔ One side of your body is completely on the mat.
- ✔ One of your knees is up; the other is down at a 90-degree angle.
- ✔ One of your elbows is down at 90 degrees; your other arm is up and out.

Kicking from the cat

You can attempt any number of kicks from the cat position. I recommend using low round-house kicks to attack your opponent's legs. Kick from the cat by following these simple steps:

1. **Maintain distance with your legs.**

   Keep your hands up to block strikes.

2. **Extend your hip as you push your raised leg with the ball of your foot into your opponent's leg.**

3. **You can also sweep your raised leg to strike the back of your opponent's leg.**

   Raise your elbow up to your palm for more distance.

4. **With a burst of energy and a push with your arm that's on the ground, you can strike your opponent's chest or head.**

Escaping from the cat

You can't stay in the cat position forever if you expect to win a fight. When you're in the cat and see a clear opportunity to stand up, use the following technique:

1. **Post your downed arm with your palm to the mat.**

   Your *downed arm* is the arm that you're leaning on the mat. Keep a hand up to protect your face.

2. **With your bottom leg, post your foot underneath your butt.**

   Think surfing stance.

3. **Keep an arm extended to protect your-self from strikes**

4. **Swing your legs back as you stand up to fighting stance.**

   See Chapter 4 for pointers on forming a strong, centered fighting stance.

Monkey Business

The monkey isn't a core position like the turtle, dog, or cat (all of which are described earlier in this chapter). Rather, it's a roll maneuver you can employ when you want to move out of the dog position. Use it any time you want to reverse your position. The following steps show how you can use the monkey roll to move from the dog position to a submission hold on your opponent's leg.

1. **From the dog position, move your arm in between both of your legs.**

2. **Roll onto your head and shoulder and end with your back to the mat.**

   You're hoping to force your opponent to roll over you. Always roll toward your up knee.

3. **As you roll onto your back, grab hold of your opponent's ankle.**

   Or use your momentum to move to a dominant position.

4. **Bring up both knees around the leg and grip the ankle with both hands to perform a knee bar hold for submission.**

Snaking Your Way to Victory

The snake is more of a maneuver than a core position. Use it when the action in a fight has slowed down. Who knows? Sometimes you can even win a fight by becoming a snake when you grapple.

1. **With your opponent mounting you and you in the guard position, lock your hands behind his back with a long grip.**

2. **Pull your hips out from under him. Tuck your chin to your chest and round your back.**

   Here, I'm sliding my body out but maintaining my grip.

3. **Keep your arms locked and obtain the dominant position of getting on your opponent's back.**

4. **Finish with a rear choke.**

   See Chapter 9 for details on how to apply a rear choke.

Part IV
Becoming a Well-Rounded Fighter — And Person

The 5th Wave   By Rich Tennant

"As a bonus to our customers, we're throwing in a wrist-lock, a neck breaker, and a stomp-to-the-groin, free of charge."

In this part . . .

Becoming a good mixed martial artist isn't just about mastering maneuvers. You also have to take good care of your body and keep it in peak fighting condition through focused training. In this part, I give you the tools you need to strengthen and condition your body. I also introduce you to several games and drills so you can train effectively and safely.

Chapter 12

Strength and Conditioning

In This Chapter

▶ Stretching to improve your flexibility

▶ Training your heart, brain, and other muscles

▶ Eating right and getting rest

*B*eing a mixed martial arts (MMA) athlete requires discipline in the areas of increasing your flexibility, practicing good nutrition, strengthening your cardiovascular system, improving your endurance, and engaging in mental training. It also means knowing when to give yourself a break to let your body recover. In this chapter, I present the basics of how to take care of your mind and body. (If you're looking for specific training routines, check out Chapter 13.)

Increasing Your Flexibility

Many MMA spectators may not realize how important flexibility is in the art of fighting. A stretched muscle is more relaxed and therefore can spring to action with greater power and intensity. Stretching also allows for increased blood flow, which in turn helps the body to recover.

The two main types of stretching are dynamic and static, as described in the following sections. I suggest you incorporate both of 'em into your conditioning program.

Dynamic stretching

Dynamic stretching consists of slow, controlled movements through the full range of motion and is best performed as a warm-up to training and fighting. Choose specific dynamic stretches that target the muscle groups you'll be using that day. For instance, if you're planning to work on the guard (covered in Chapter 7), stretch your lower back, hips, and calves. If you're going to be kickboxing, stretch your hamstrings, hips, and shoulders.

Following are some examples of dynamic stretching, starting from the shoulders on down:

- **Shoulder circles:** Make circles with your shoulders by moving them up and rolling them back down.

- **Arm swings:** Swing your arms forward and backward. Also, swing your arms out to your sides and across your chest.

- **Hip circles:** With your feet wider than your shoulders, rotate your hips in a clockwise direction.

- **Leg swings:** Swing your leg backward and forward. Do 10 to 12 repetitions before switching legs.

- **Standing groin stretches:** Take a wide stance and keep your arms straight in front of you for balance. Lunge to your left, bending your left leg and straightening your right leg. Now do the same on the opposite side.

- **Lunges:** Start standing with both feet together. Keep your back straight as you lunge forward with your left leg. Your left thigh should be parallel to the floor, and your left lower leg should be vertical. Hold the lunge for about 30 seconds and return to your starting position. Repeat with your other leg.

✔ **Downward dog to cat stretch:** From the dog position (which I describe in Chapter 11), raise your butt and straighten your legs with your palms still to the mat. From this downward dog position, lower your elbows as you arch your back forward. End with your hips to the mat and your gaze looking up. Repeat.

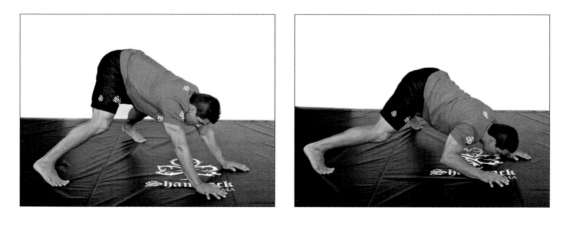

Static stretching

Static stretching is when you stretch your muscles while they're relaxed. Static stretches are best performed during the cool-down period after you train or fight. Be sure to target the muscle groups you used that day.

Check out these examples of static stretching:

✔ **Groin stretch:** Sit tall and ease your legs up to your body. Place the soles of your feet together. With your knees to your sides, rest your hands on your lower legs and ease your knees to the ground. You'll feel the stretch along the inside of your thighs and groin.

✔ **Shoulder stretch:** Stand tall with your feet slightly wider than shoulder width apart. Bring your right arm parallel to the floor and across your chest. Use your left arm to bend up and ease your right arm closer to your chest. Hold for 30 seconds, release, change sides, and repeat.

Pumping Up That Blood Flow: Cardiovascular Training

Your heart, veins, and lungs work in unison to fuel your body. That's why *cardiovascular training,* which involves getting your heart rate up to stimulate blood flow, is paramount in keeping your vitals strong and your body in tip-top condition.

Work your cardiovascular system for at least 20 minutes, three days a week, making sure to keep your heart rate up and within your target zone this entire time. Your full workout should last 30 minutes with 5 minutes each for warming up and cooling down.

You can achieve your target heart rate any number of ways, including by

- **Running:** This activity is the best way to work your cardiovascular system. You don't need any fancy equipment other than a decent pair of shoes, and getting started is just a matter of stepping outside. (Of course, if you have access to a treadmill, using that is fine too.) The impact of running can be tough on your joints though, so be sure not to overextend yourself if you start feeling any stiffness in your knees.

- **Bicycling:** Whether you're on a stationary bike or you're cycling through the great outdoors, bicycling can give you a great cardio workout without the pressure on your knees, hips, and other joints that you can get with running.

- **Elliptical training:** Because your feet never leave the pedals, elliptical machines make for a cardio workout that's low-impact and easy on your joints.

- **Cross-country skiing:** For the best cardiovascular results with the least amount of negative impact, try cross-country skiing. This activity uses the muscle groups in your shoulders, back, chest, butt, abdomen, and legs to provide a complete body workout.

Ultimately, you simply need to find a heart rate–raising cardio activity that works for you, your schedule, and your surroundings.

Determining your target heart rate

Your *target heart rate* — which you want to hit for your workouts to be as effective as possible — is a range within 60 percent to 75 percent of your maximum heart rate (MHR). A quick search of the Internet presents you with numerous calculators for finding your target heart rate, but it's actually pretty easy to figure out for yourself if you don't have a computer or Internet-equipped phone handy. (And seriously, who does at the gym?)

Start by taking your pulse to find your resting heart rate (RHR). Simply run the index and middle fingers of your right hand down your left thumb and press down approximately an inch below your wrist until you feel your pulse. Watch a clock for exactly 60 seconds and count how many times your pulse beats during that time. Tada! You've just figured out your personal RHR.

To find your target heart rate, take it one step further by applying this formula:

220 − Your age − Your RHR × .60 + Your RHR = _____ 60% MHR

220 − Your age − Your RHR × .75 + Your RHR = _____ 75% MHR

So if you're 20 years old and your RHR is 60, your target heart rate is 144 to 165 beats per minute.

The easiest way to know whether your heart rate is up is by performing the *talk test*. In the middle of your workout, try to say a sentence aloud. If you can say the sentence easily and comfortably, you aren't working hard enough. Of course, you may also want to invest in a heart rate monitor so you can more accurately monitor whether you're staying within your target heart rate.

Building Your Endurance

Given the combined elements of a controlled pace and the explosive speed and power necessary in MMA, proper endurance training is essential. It builds muscle mass and makes your muscles strong, giving you power and helping you avoid injury. Make endurance training a part of your routine training regimen and be sure to do it more frequently whenever you're preparing for a fight.

Losing a fight to a better opponent is acceptable, but losing a fight because you're tired indicates a lack of preparation and inadequate training. To avoid such a scenario, make sure you take your heart and muscle endurance well beyond what it will ever be asked to do in a fight. For example, if you can do 30 minutes of hard cardio without getting fatigued, you'll be in good condition to breeze through a 15-minute match without tiring. And when you don't get tired, you can think more clearly under pressure, listen to your corner, and be able to perform the strategy and technique you trained for.

To build up your endurance, start training within your target heart rate for 30 minutes, four or five times a week. After about four weeks, recheck your resting heart rate to see whether it has decreased. If it has, that's an indication that your heart is now in better condition and can pump more blood throughout your body in fewer beats per minute.

When it comes to specific endurance exercises, use your own body weight to build muscle mass. Twice a week I do five sets of endurance exercises such as squats, dips, push-ups, pull-ups, and leg lifts. (For more information on how to do these exercises, see *Workouts For Dummies* by Tamilee Webb and Lori Seeger [Wiley].) Start with a number of repetitions that you can do comfortably and add five more repetitions per set of each exercise each time you work out.

Swimming is also a great endurance activity that uses your whole body. Because it's low-impact, it's a great cross-training activity for an MMA fighter.

Keeping Things Interesting: Interval Training

Over time, your body will naturally grow accustomed to your training regimen and you'll stop noticing improvements in your workouts. To avoid slipping into this status quo mode for long, you need to start incorporating the interval training necessary for the explosive nature of MMA. Effective interval training involves going beyond the upper range of your target heart rate for brief periods of time during your cardiovascular training.

Try running within your target heart rate for 30 minutes, sprinting every fifth minute to raise your heart rate to between 80 and 85 percent of your maximum heart rate. Drop back down into your target zone for four minutes, and then sprint again for an entire minute. Loosen your muscles and run as fast as you can for that minute. Repeat these intervals for 30 minutes. You can also apply this concept to elliptical machines and stationary bikes. No matter which of these activities you choose, this type of training prepares you for those many intervals in a fight when you must explode by firing off punches quickly or by throwing knee and kick combinations.

Be sure to warm up and cool down with brisk walking five minutes before and after your interval training sessions. Doing so reduces the effects of blood pooling in the joints (which can cause soreness) and allows your heart to safely return to its regular rhythm.

Revving Up Your Resistance Training

In *resistance training,* also called strength training, your peripheral muscles push or pull against some force. This force can be gravity, such as when you lift weights at a health club or when you lift part of your own weight in a push-up. Or your muscles can work against another force, like when you use a rowing machine. Over time and with repeated activity, muscle fibers become longer and thicker. Subsequently, you're able to work against a greater force (in other words, lift heavier weights) for longer periods of time.

It may sound like a lot of work, but adding just 60 minutes per week (three 20-minute sessions, for example) of resistance training to your current training regimen is all you need to begin seeing benefits. Following these guidelines will also put you well on your way to resistance-training success:

✔ Talk to your doctor before you begin any type of resistance-training program.

✔ Begin your resistance training with a 10 to 15 minute aerobic warm-up to increase the blood flow throughout your body and loosen stiff joints.

✔ Tight muscles are easily strained, so stretch the regions you plan to exercise. Hold stretches for approximately 30 seconds and repeat each stretch at least once. (For specific stretch ideas, see the "Dynamic stretching" and "Static stretching" sections earlier in this chapter.)

✔ Make resistance training enjoyable by not lifting excessively heavy weights. An appropriate level of effort should allow you to comfortably lift a weight repetitively at least 12 to 15 times for two to three sets.

✔ Hit all the big muscle groups first (chest, upper back, abdominals, buttocks, hamstrings, and thighs). Then target the smaller groups (biceps, triceps, forearms, shoulders, and calves).

✔ Focus on correct form and not on the amount of weight you can lift.

✔ Don't swing your back to help you lift additional weight. Consider using a support belt for your lower back.

✔ Always breathe naturally.

✔ Consult a personal trainer to show you proper lifting techniques and the most effective exercises for any particular muscle group.

Getting Proper Nutrition

The type of nutritional plan you develop really depends on your personal goals. For example, the diet of someone who wants to gain weight for a fight is entirely different from the diet of a fighter who needs to cut weight.

If you want to maintain your weight *and* nourish your body while in training mode,

- ✔ **Eat at least five meals a day.** Some fighters eat as many as six to eight meals a day. Each meal should be the size of your clenched fist and contain vegetables and complex carbohydrates from live sources. Complex carbohydrates provide a steady source of energy. I'm a fan of oatmeal, bran, corn, yams, carrots, potatoes, beans, and lentils.

- ✔ **Drink lots and lots of water.** Water aids in the process of converting stored fat into energy. Keeping yourself hydrated is essential every day, not just when you're training. So get in the habit of drinking a gallon of water a day.

- ✔ **Don't let supplements and protein shakes stand in for a good diet.** Yes, supplements and shakes are a good way to get essential nutrients, but the best way to score key nutrients for your body is to get them from live sources. Build a good habit of eating healthy food and only use vitamins, supplements, and shakes to add to your already healthy diet.

If you need help with the basics of good nutrition, see *Nutrition For Dummies,* 4th Edition, written by Carol Ann Rinzler and published by Wiley.

Flexing Your Mental Muscles

Your mind is a powerful tool. Even when your body is tired from exhaustive workouts, you can keep training mentally. Think about techniques abstractly and mechanically. Draw them. Write them down, step by step. Talk to someone about the power of angles found in submissions. Any of these activities plants information in your brain so it can be called upon when needed.

Additionally, you can keep your mind active and strong and your spirit positive with the three core levels of mental training: meditation, hypnosis, and visual training.

Meditation

Meditation allows you to both focus and relax. Here's a basic technique:

1. **Find a place that's clear of distractions.**

   A quiet, dark, comfortable spot is key. Soothing music and smells are nice, but they aren't a necessity.

2. **Relax and clear your mind.**

3. **Focus on your breath.**

   Extend and lengthen your breath.

4. **Fix your thoughts.**

   Breathe in and think positive. Think of a technique you want to master in training. Breathe out and release any negative thoughts or problems.

Hypnosis

Hypnosis is an extension of meditation. If meditation is like erasing a chalkboard and clearing the mind, hypnosis is like writing on that chalkboard. While meditating, write on that chalkboard anything you want your mind to believe. If you think it, your mind believes it and that task gets done.

Visual training

Visual training is an extension of hypnosis and the third level of the mental training process. When your mind is clear, walk through and visualize techniques in your mind. Doing so trains your mind to believe that you did the technique. And if you think it, you can do it.

Start small. Visualize an angle or the first step in attempting a submission hold. If you have a hard time visualizing, go back to meditating and clear your mind.

Healing and Getting Rest

Think of rest as a serious part of your training regimen. In a perfect world, you'd be able to nap after every training session. But if you don't have the time for such rest, be sure to get at least eight hours of sleep a night.

Listen to your body. If it doesn't want to work out, don't force it to.

If you're training hard, you're going to experience aches and pains. The most immediate way to treat these minor ailments is through *cryotherapy,* which is really just a fancy way of saying you should use ice to treat pain and inflammation. Here are some general guidelines:

- ✔ Use ice on small joints for 10 minutes.
- ✔ Use ice on medium joints for 15 to 20 minutes.
- ✔ Use ice on large joints for 20 to 30 minutes.

Obviously, if you're in great pain or feel that some part of you is seriously out of whack, see your trainer or a physician. As a fighter, you always feel like you have to tough things out, but if you're injured, get treated. Sometimes it's hard to tell whether that twinge in your knee is just a bruise or, as you may fear, a torn ligament. The best approach is to get it checked out. After all, the sooner you get treated, the sooner you can go back to training.

The following injuries always require treatment by a physician. Don't just try to walk them off and hope you'll feel better the next day. See a doctor. Why risk permanent injury?

- ✔ Neck or back pain
- ✔ Loss of consciousness after taking a blow to the head

Chapter 13

Training with a Purpose

- -

In This Chapter

▶ Turning practice into playtime with training games

▶ Using a ball to enhance your balance and control

▶ Working on training drills to improve your skills

- -

*I*f you want to get the most from your training, playing games and practicing drills are safer than *sparring* (free-form fighting) with someone at your training facility. Why? Because games and drills are controlled and focused on developing certain techniques, not trying to inflict damage on someone. Consequently, games and drills can improve your performance of specific techniques, such as takedowns, submission holds, and more. In this chapter, I present numerous games you can try, as well as tips for using an exercise ball in your training and several drills you can perform alone or with a partner.

Turning Your Training into a Game

Training games are a great, safe way to target specific areas of fighting that require development. They allow you to both vary your training regimen and make it a bit more competitive.

You must have a partner to perform these games. Don't try to do them on your own. Also, be sure to adequately warm up before you start any training game. (For some effective warm-ups, check out Chapter 12.)

Balance and control game

Break the balance and control game out when you want to work on developing your motor skills for balance and control, or simply when you want to strengthen your position and escape techniques.

- ✔ **How to play:** You can start the balance and control game in any position. Whoever's on top may use only one hand for holding or control and only his body weight and position to stay on top.

- ✔ **Ways to win:** The bottom person wins if he can escape the position and get on top or into fighting stance.

- ✔ **Variations:** If you're on top, try holding your partner without using your hands.

Dog game

The dog game helps you develop full lower-body strength, build up your arm strength, and improve your escape from and timing of the dog position. Whoever's on top during the game gets the added benefit of developing balance and control.

- ✔ **How to play:** The game starts with the bottom person in dog position (see Chapter 11). The top person is behind him in a wrestler's referee type of position (think one hand on your partner's elbow and one across his stomach). Both partners must maintain the dog position.

- ✔ **Ways to win:** The bottom person must escape to his feet to win. The top person wins if the time expires and he's still holding the position. Times are variable. I recommend 20 seconds to start; then bump it up by increments of 10 seconds.

- ✔ **Variations:** If you want to change things up a bit, make it so that the bottom person must escape *and* be unattached from his partner in order to win. If you have more people, try playing this game like a tournament with the winner staying in.

Leg game

The best part about the leg game is that it encourages full lower-body strengthening and enhances your ability to obtain the leg submission position. It also helps you practice your leg blocking and attacking. So grab a partner and get started!

- ✔ **How to play:** The leg game starts with you and your partner on your backs with your legs intertwined. Both of you should have one leg on each side of your body. Don't attempt any submission holds; they aren't allowed in this game.

- ✔ **Ways to win:** Both participants can win at this game. To win, you must achieve leg position completely (meaning your feet are together, your knees are together at a 90-degree angle, and you're on your side).

- ✔ **Variations:** To change this game up, simply wear pants or shoes. You can also start the game in the leg position and work backward so that you have to escape from the leg position in order to win.

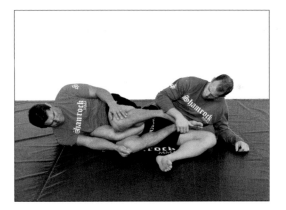

Choke game

Playing the choke game helps you work on neck strengthening and raises your comfort level in escaping a choke hold (I present several in Chapter 9).

- ✔ **How to play:** Start by sitting on the mat, facing your partner's back. Wrap your legs and arms around him to achieve the choke position. Then pull your partner on top of your body and set up all the elements of the choke position, except for the choke itself.

- ✔ **Ways to win:** If the choke is set and your partner taps out, you win. If your partner gets back to the mat, he wins.

- ✔ **Variations:** Alternate between long and short chokes. When you've grown more comfortable with the choke, you can play this game by setting the choke and then attempting to escape it.

Clinch game

The clinch game is a great one for fully conditioning your body and improving your hand-eye coordination. *Note:* You definitely want to wear your protective gear (headgear, kneepads, gloves, elbow pads, and a mouthpiece) when playing this game.

- ✔ **How to play:** From the clinch, try to strike your partner without being struck. If you see a strike coming, move out of the way.

- ✔ **Ways to win:** Winning this game is simple — don't get struck by your partner!

- ✔ **Variations:** Try throwing only punches, kicks, or knees.

Position game

Playing the position game allows you to get comfortable in the various positions without the worry of potential submissions.

- ✔ **How to play:** Pick any of the eight positions and decide to either stay in that position or try to get out of it. Based on your decision, your partner will either try to get you out of that position or force you to stay in it. For example, say you decide to try to keep the guard position (described in Chapter 7). In this case, your partner will try to get you out of your guard.

- ✔ **Ways to win:** You can win the position game by either maintaining the position you chose or defending against your partner's choice of position.

- ✔ **Variations:** Simply choose a different position each time you play.

Bettering Your Balance with Ball Training

The ball is a unique tool to add to your training and conditioning. It's perfect for helping you find balance and control and maintaining your center through any movement. You can find a ball at any sporting goods store. Pick one on which you can sit comfortably with your thighs parallel to the ground.

When you first start training with a ball, you're going to have a hard time with balance, so wear a helmet and pads and use a spotter. If you don't, you may fall off the ball and injure yourself. Also, be sure to consult with your doctor before beginning this type of training.

Before kicking off any ball-training session, always take time to warm up your core, back, and hips.

Sitting on the ball

Having a seat on your ball is quite a bit more difficult than it sounds. Sitting on a ball and staying put requires practice and focus. However, mastering this exercise helps you develop balance and core strength. Here's how you do it:

1. **Sit on the ball and lift your feet.**

2. **Try to balance all of your body weight on the ball for 20 seconds.**

   After you've mastered 20 seconds, add comfortable increments of time up to the 2-minute range.

3. **If you fall off, keep trying.**

Getting up on your knees

This exercise requires some serious balance, and you definitely need a spotter to get in position.

1. **With the help of a spotter (or maybe two), get up on your knees on the ball.**

2. **Hold your arms out and try to stay balanced for 20 seconds.**

Practicing positions on the ball

Use the ball as you would a partner and flow through the series of eight positions that I present in Chapter 8. Here are a few examples:

Head and arm hold:

The mount:

Leg hold:

You can even practice your guard technique.

Drilling to Develop Your Technique

The following drills aid in the development of various fighting techniques. All of 'em should be done in repetitions (ideally three sets of five repetitions each). If the drills require a partner, be sure to do your set and then switch roles with your partner.

I recommend you do three to five drills a day, three to five times a week. Alternate the drills each week. For instance, work on takedown techniques such as the double leg, sweep, and sprawl one week, and escape techniques such as the monkey roll, shrimp, and sit out the following week.

Boxer twist

The boxer twist is a great warm-up to do on your own before any stand-up fighting training session. It works your torso and gets you on the balls of your feet; it also prepares you for the movement involved in stand-up fighting.

1. **Start with your elbows up and your knees bent.**
2. **Bring your right fist and your left fist up above your chin, with knuckles touching.**
3. **Standing on the balls of your feet, twist your body from side to side, making sure to keep your center.**

   Don't lean backward or forward.

Parry punch

The parry punch is the drill to try if you want to get more comfortable parrying punches. Grab a partner and do the following:

- ✔ Using whichever hand is closest to your partner's punch, slightly slap the punch away from your face.
- ✔ Keep your head away from the hand that's parrying your partner's punch.

Punch catch

Instead of slapping your partner's punch away like in the parry punch drill (described in the preceding section), the punch catch drill calls for you to catch your partner's punch in your hand. Simply stand with your partner and catch his punch before it hits your face.

Bridge

The bridge is one of the most commonly used escapes in grappling, and this drill can help you perform it seamlessly. *Note:* You can do this drill solo. Here's how:

1. **Start on your back with your hands up, elbows in, and shoulders shrugged.**
2. **Looking toward the mat, bridge on your head and shoulder and push your hips up toward the ceiling.**

   For step-by-step instructions on forming the bridge, see Chapter 10.

Bridge off wall

To further strengthen your bridge-forming skills, run through the bridge off wall drill with a partner. Start off by having your partner stand while you assume the turtle position (which I present in Chapter 11).

1. **Place your feet on your partner's thighs.**
2. **Push off of your feet, raise your butt, and arch your back into the bridge.**

   Turn to Chapter 10 for the basics of the bridge.

3. **Look over your shoulder.**
4. **Drop down and switch sides.**

Elevator mat drill

Perform the elevator mat drill on your own when you want to strengthen your escape techniques in ground fighting.

1. **Start in the turtle position.**

   Flip to Chapter 11 for the basics of the turtle.

2. **Elevate your arms and legs on one side of your body and drop to the mat.**

3. **Lock your head and hip and roll over so that you're now in the dog position.**

   If you're in a proper dog position, you should be on all fours, as explained in Chapter 11.

Shrimp mat drill

Do this drill solo to work on the movement of the shrimp technique. (You can see how to use the shrimp as an escape in Chapter 10.)

1. **From your back, get onto your side.**

2. **Push off the balls of your feet, reach your fingers to your toes, and scoot your butt out.**

3. **Switch sides and repeat.**

Pummeling

Pummeling is used as part of the clinch in stand-up fighting. (You can see it used in Chapter 5.) This is one drill you definitely need to practice with a partner.

1. **Start in the clinch with your partner.**

2. **Swim one of your arms under his arm as your other arm swims over his other arm.**

3. **Bump your chest with your partner's chest on the side where you swam your arm under.**

Shoulder shuck

The shoulder shuck is an escape from the clinch (presented in Chapter 5). Grab a partner and follow these instructions for running this drill:

1. **Start in the clinch position with your partner.**

2. **Pinch his wrist between your head and shoulder.**

3. **Let go of your partner's head as you twist your torso.**

4. **Rotate and push the arm controlling your head and point it toward the mat.**

Guard sit-up drill

You can do this drill solo to work on the guard sit-up position covered in Chapter 7.

1. **From the turtle position, drop to one side.**

   If you're unsure how to form the turtle, see Chapter 11.

2. **Double-check your body positioning.**

   Your bottom leg and top leg should be at 90 degrees, and you should be on the ball of your foot. Your downed elbow should be at 90 degrees. Finally, your chest should be out with your back straight and your fist at your chest.

3. **Return to turtle, switch sides, and repeat.**

Dog stand up to fighting stance drill

When you want to practice getting into a centered fighting stance from the dog position, perform this drill solo.

1. **From the dog position, stand up and turn your up knee down toward the mat.**

   When in dog position, you're on all fours. Turn to Chapter 11 for the specifics on this position.

2. **Look up toward the opposite direction of your up knee as you stand up to fighting stance.**

Sit out and follow

Sitting out is a useful escape technique. Practice this drill on your own to enhance your sitting out skills.

1. **From the dog position, sit out and return to dog.**

   See Chapter 10 for direction on how to sit out.

2. **Perform a dog stand up, looking up toward the opposite direction of your up knee as you stand up to fighting stance.**

Kick and turn drill

You can use the kick and turn drill to practice roundhouse kicks on your own.

1. **From fighting stance, step off on the ball of your foot.**

   Check out Chapter 4 for a review of the core components of a strong stand-up fighting stance.

2. **Kick all the way around and land in fighting stance.**

   Switch the leg you kick with after each set.

Switch and turn drill

Want to improve your switch kick? Perform this solo switch and turn drill as follows:

1. **From fighting stance, perform a switch kick.**

   See Chapter 4 for pointers on switch kicks.

2. **Spin all the way around on the ball of your foot.**

3. **Land in fighting stance.**

Pyramid drill

The pyramid drill helps you develop balance and control. You don't need a partner for this one.

1. **From the dog position, reach your hands out farther than your shoulders.**

   Flip to Chapter 11 for some pointers on forming the dog.

2. **Place your forehead to the mat.**

3. **Lift your knees off the ground and raise your butt into the air.**

Part V
The Part of Tens

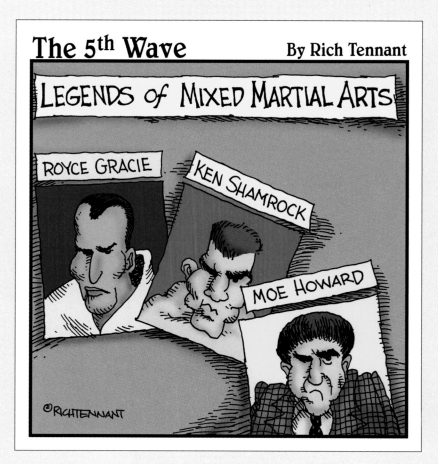

The 5th Wave   By Rich Tennant

LEGENDS of MIXED MARTIAL ARTS

ROYCE GRACIE

KEN SHAMROCK

MOE HOWARD

In this part . . .

Who doesn't enjoy a good Top Ten list — or three? These chapters present the ten best ways to improve your speed and prepare for a fight, as well as ten surefire ways to get yourself hurt. (After all, you're far less likely to get injured if you know what not to do.)

Chapter 14

Ten Ways to Improve Your Speed

Speed can be the difference between winning or losing a fight in mixed martial arts (MMA). Improving your speed involves maintaining good technique, keeping up with physical activity, enhancing your hand-eye coordination, and watching out for your physical well-being. Fortunately, you have a variety of options available for each of these things — some of which may surprise you.

Practice Good Technique

If you maintain good technique, you'll always be fast. It's as simple as that.

Every technique presented in this book is proven to work in the quickest, most direct way possible. For zeroing in on speed, make sure to use your angles when you train and fight. Keeping yourself at a 45-degree angle from your opponent gives you speed because it cuts down the distance between you.

Work the Speed Bag

The speed bag has traditionally been used as a training tool for boxing, but it's also quite effective for helping you punch up your MMA skills. Many MMA gyms have a speed bag, and if used properly, it can be a great way to increase your speed.

To use a speed bag properly, just focus on control and remember to hit the bag on odd intervals. Hit it first on count one, let it bounce and rebound on the second count, and then hit it again on count three. Work slow with circle punches until you create a good rhythm. Then you can start moving faster and adding in combinations.

Take a Dip: Water Training

One of my favorite cross-training activities is swimming. Along with doing laps, I like to replicate punches, combos, and kicks underwater. The water resistance impacts your full range of motion, resulting in added strength and fluidity of movement.

Jump Rope

Explosive exercises, such as jumping rope, have long been a mixed martial artist's tool for improving speed. Jumping rope at short bursts and high speeds develops your fast twitch muscle fibers, which means your muscles will contract more quickly when you need them.

Hang Ten

You probably can't picture your favorite MMA fighter hangin' ten, but surfing can actually be very beneficial. Surfing requires a great sense of balance, which is also a necessary MMA skill. Improving your balance allows you to react more readily in competition.

Improve Your Flexibility

Increased flexibility enhances both your speed and range of motion. Yoga, which is all about stretching and growing your flexibility, is a practice I find most rewarding for its spiritual and healing aspects. Focusing on your center, which is vital in MMA and a priority in yoga, strengthens your core and maintains balance in your spine and musculature.

Play Video Games

There's no need to get sucked into *World of Warcraft* for the sake of obtaining quicker submission holds, but playing some video games can definitely improve your speed. Why? Because video games are known to enhance hand-eye coordination. So pick up that controller and get your *Metroid* on!

Juggle

Forget the face paint and the big red nose. Believe it or not, juggling can be a very serious tool for helping improve your speed. Much like playing video games, juggling improves your hand-eye coordination, a staple skill in anyone's MMA bag o' tricks.

Lose Weight

Carrying less weight on your person allows you to move more quickly. Focus on losing excess fat through nutritional planning and exercise. (I offer some tips on both in Chapter 12.)

Sleep

Never overlook the importance of rest. A taxed, tired body is a slow one, so make sure to get at least eight hours of sleep each night.

Chapter 15

Ten Ways to Get Yourself Hurt

*Y*ou've seen it time and time again: fighters injuring themselves during training or before an important fight. Chances are good they did one of the following ten things to get themselves hurt. Avoid their mistakes by recognizing (and avoiding!) these guaranteed causes of injury.

Closing Your Eyes or Looking Away

Everyone blinks, but if you close your eyes for more than a blink, you're asking to get hurt. Be aware of your opponent and don't let your eyes wander to other distractions.

Dropping Your Hands

Dropping your hands is a telltale sign that you're an amateur fighter rather than an experienced one. Always keep your hands up to protect your face.

Passing on Your Warm-up

Warming up is absolutely essential if you want to avoid injury. Warming up the muscles and increasing blood flow decreases muscle stiffness, which is a common cause of injury.

Failing to Stretch

Stretching improves your range of motion. Stretching before training or competition allows you to apply a technique that requires a longer range of motion without the risk of injury.

Skipping Out on Conditioning

If you compete without proper conditioning, you *will* get hurt. Getting tired in the ring is often what causes a loss by knockout or technical knockout. Your movements become slower and your reaction time suffers, giving your opponent the opportunity to inflict damage.

Forgetting to Breathe

Breathing is a very important practice that many beginning MMA fighters forget to maintain. Your every movement should begin and end with a focused breath. Panic can lead to hyper-ventilation, so always stay relaxed and focused while in competition by maintaining that steady, focused breath.

Not Tapping When You Feel Pain

Failing to tap is one of the most common causes of injury in mixed martial arts. Show respect for your opponent and yourself by tapping the moment you feel pain. It's best to tap your opponent's body with a succession of taps. However, if you can't reach his body, you can tap the mat or verbally call out. See Chapter 3 for more on when and how to tap.

Neglecting to Wear Protection

Whether in competition or training, wearing the necessary protective gear is extremely important. Wear your mouthpiece, cup, headgear, hand wraps, and gloves whenever you spar.

Overtraining

Not allowing your body adequate rest can result in injury. By training too much, you can strain your body, tear muscles, or put stress on your joints.

Resting your body is just as important as strengthening and conditioning it.

Using Bad Technique

If you maintain bad technique, you're guaranteed to hurt yourself. A technique as simple as the fighting stance (presented in Chapter 4) can be done poorly by not staying centered or by crossing your feet. Mistakes like these can be costly. Strive to maintain good technique at all times.

Chapter 16

Ten Ways to Prepare for a Fight

In This Chapter

▶ Knowing what to do in the weeks leading up to your fight

▶ Getting your body ready to go right before hopping into the ring

*Y*ou've trained and trained for this moment — a scheduled fight. Follow these steps to make sure you're adequately prepared so you can perform at your best.

Prime Your Body for the Rounds

Be prepared for the timed rounds by getting in shape. Usually rounds last five minutes, with one-minute rests in between. Title fights generally go five rounds, whereas nontitle matches go three rounds. Structure your training schedule with timed, explosive workouts to familiarize yourself with the rounds.

Drink Lots of Water

After you know you have a fight coming, you should always carry water with you. Strive to drink a gallon each day and be sure to keep yourself hydrated during workouts.

Get to Know Your Opponent

Study your opponent however you can. If you can access tapes of his fights, watch all of 'em. Train with the people who've fought or trained with him. Figuring out all you can about your opponent's strengths and weaknesses can help you decide on a strategy for the fight.

Obtain Clearance from Your Doctor

You can't fight without your doctor's permission, so make sure you contact him or her for clearance as soon as you know you'll be fighting. This involves scheduling a physical that will likely include an eye exam, an EKG, and a blood test.

Signed medical clearance lasts up to one year. For more specifics, look into the athletic commission's rules for the state you're fighting in (each state has its own rules).

Develop a Diet Plan

Create a solid diet plan to prepare you for the fight. Your diet should include water, lots of vegetables, and plenty of complex carbohydrates.

Stick to Your Training Program

In the weeks leading up to your fight, don't deter from your focused training program. Instead, be sure to condition yourself well and study techniques that can attack your opponent's weaknesses or counter his strengths.

Rest

Remember to rest as part of your training program. Get at least eight hours of sleep each night and, if time permits, rest after each training session.

You should stop training and rest for five days before your scheduled fight. You don't want to fight with a sore and tired body. You must rest before a fight so you can compete with a refreshed and revitalized body and mind.

Meditate

Practice meditation during your five-day prefight rest period. Focus specifically on breathing out any fears or insecurities and visualize victory. Chapter 12 has tips that can help you with visualization.

Warm Up

Warming up your muscles before a fight is paramount. I suggest shadowboxing, light mitt work and pummeling, and general calisthenics. When at the fight location, be sure to stay warm backstage leading up to the fight. Also, keep moving when you're in the ring waiting for the fight to begin.

Stretch

As part of your warm-up, perform *dynamic stretches* (slow, controlled movements that use your full range of motion). Flip to Chapter 12 for ideas on different dynamic stretches you can try.

Appendix

Resources

· ·

*W*ant to find out more about MMA? Check out some of the resources featured in this appendix. I list Shamrock Submission Fighting–certified teachers if you're interested in finding an MMA trainer and school. You can also keep up to date with my whereabouts on my Web sites and social networking pages. And don't hesitate to connect with me and other MMA fans on Internet forums and message boards.

Professional Organizations

National Association of Professional Martial Artists (NAPMA): www.napma.com

Martial Arts Teachers Association (MATA): www.martialartsteachers.com

Shamrock Submission Fighting Instructors

Arizona

Chris Blier, SSF Level II
Location: Phoenix, AZ
E-mail: cblieraz@gmail.com

John Nottingham, SSF Level II
USA Martial Arts
Location: Scottsdale, AZ
Phone: 480-443-0088
E-mail: info@usa-martialarts.com
Web site: www.usa-martialarts.com

Arkansas

Lee Gyung, SSF Level I
ATA Blackbelt Leadership Academy
Phone: 501-753-6100
E-mail: myatakarate@hotmail.com
Web site: www.myatakarate.com

Norman Trey Vaden, SSF Level II
Razorback Fight Club
Location: Wynne, AR
Phone: 870-208-9796
E-mail: trey_vaden@yahoo.com
Web site: www.myspace.com/treyvaden

California

Dana and Jackie Charvet, SSF Level I
Danger Zone MMA
Location: Oxnard, CA
Phone: 805-382-1310
E-mail: dangerzonemma@msn.com
Web site: www.dangerzonemma.org

Jake Shannon, SSF Level II
Scientific Wrestling
Phone: 310-228-7175
E-mail: training@scientificwrestling.com
Web site: www.scientificwrestling.com

Nevada

Reggie Cochran, SSF National Director
Henderson, NV
Phone: 702-898-3171
E-mail: blackbeltsuccess@aol.com
Web site: www.reggiecochran.com

New Jersey

Dusty Everson, SSF Level I
Everson's Karate
Location: Robbinsville, NJ
Phone: 609-448-1807
Web site: www.eversons.com

Paul Prendergast, SSF Level II
Paul Prendergast Karate
Location: Brick, NJ
Phone: 732-477-8451
E-mail: MasterPaulP@aol.com
Web site: www.brickkarate.com

Phil Ross, SSF Level II
American Eagle MMA & Kettlebells
Location: Ho Ho Kus, NJ
Phone: 201-612-1429
E-mail: philrossmma1@gmail.com
Web site: www.philross.com

North Carolina

Ryan Hoover, SSF Level I
Location: Charlotte, NC
Phone: 704-814-0300
E-mail: ryan@wearefittofight.com
Web site: www.wearefittofight.com

Pennsylvania

Joel Nott
Bloomsburg Mixed Martial Arts
Location: Bloomsburg, PA
Phone: 570-204-9991
Web site: www.bloomsubwrestling.com

Washington

Rob Eis, SSF Level II
Unbridled Martial Arts
Location: Bellingham, WA
Phone: 360-676-9909
E-mail: info@unbridledmartialarts.com
Web site: www.unbridledmartialarts.com

Wisconsin

Scott Lewandowski, SSF Level I
Location: Hartland, WI
Phone: 262-367-3595
Web site: usatkd.cmasdirect.com

United Kingdom

Jason Dorn and Selina Stayte, SSF Level I
Paragon Academy
134-136 Bath Street
Ilkeston, Derbyshire, DE7 8FF
United Kingdom
Phone: 0115 9300090
E-mail: `mail@paragonacademy.co.uk` or `jasondorn@btinternet.com`
Web site: `www.paragonacademy.co.uk`

MMA Web Sites and Community Forums

`www.sherdog.com`: MMA news, fighters' stats, and large community forum

`www.mmaweekly.com`: MMA news and rankings

`www.f4wonline.com`: Wrestling Observer, the most detailed coverage and analysis of pro wrestling and MMA

`www.fila-wrestling.com`: FILA Wrestling, international Federation of Associated Wrestling Styles

`www.themat.com`: USA Wrestling, wrestling news and message board

`www.usagrappling.com`: United States grappling news

`www.mma.tv`: MMA news and forums

`www.realfightermag.com`: *Real Fighter Magazine*

Official Frank Shamrock Web Sites

`www.shamrockmma.com`: The Web site for the Shamrock MMA schools

`www.frankshamrock.com`: My personal interactive Web site

`www.myspace.com/frankshamrock`: My MySpace page

`www.youtube.com/thefrankshamrock`: My YouTube Channel

`www.facebook.com/profile.php?id=663448273`: My Facebook page

`www.mmastars.com`: MMA Stars fighter and talent development

`shamrockathletics.com`: Shamrock Apparel

`mmaeinc.com`: Mixed Martial Arts Entertainment

Mixed Martial Arts Supplies

shamrockathletics.com: MMA supplies and apparel

swainmats.com: MMA mats

Organizations and Promotions

www.ufc.com: Ultimate Fighting Championship

www.strikeforce.com: Strikeforce

www.elitexc.com: Elite XC

Rules and Athletic Commissions

Unified Rules of Mixed Martial Arts:
www.nj.gov/lps/sacb/docs/martial.html

California State Athletic Commission: www.dca.ca.gov/csac

Index

● *T* ●

• *Y* •

BUSINESS, CAREERS & PERSONAL FINANCE

Accounting For Dummies, 4th Edition*
978-0-470-24600-9

Bookkeeping Workbook For Dummies†
978-0-470-16983-4

Commodities For Dummies
978-0-470-04928-0

Doing Business in China For Dummies
978-0-470-04929-7

E-Mail Marketing For Dummies
978-0-470-19087-6

Job Interviews For Dummies, 3rd Edition*†
978-0-470-17748-8

Personal Finance Workbook For Dummies*†
978-0-470-09933-9

Real Estate License Exams For Dummies
978-0-7645-7623-2

Six Sigma For Dummies
978-0-7645-6798-8

Small Business Kit For Dummies, 2nd Edition*†
978-0-7645-5984-6

Telephone Sales For Dummies
978-0-470-16836-3

BUSINESS PRODUCTIVITY & MICROSOFT OFFICE

Access 2007 For Dummies
978-0-470-03649-5

Excel 2007 For Dummies
978-0-470-03737-9

Office 2007 For Dummies
978-0-470-00923-9

Outlook 2007 For Dummies
978-0-470-03830-7

PowerPoint 2007 For Dummies
978-0-470-04059-1

Project 2007 For Dummies
978-0-470-03651-8

QuickBooks 2008 For Dummies
978-0-470-18470-7

Quicken 2008 For Dummies
978-0-470-17473-9

Salesforce.com For Dummies, 2nd Edition
978-0-470-04893-1

Word 2007 For Dummies
978-0-470-03658-7

EDUCATION, HISTORY, REFERENCE & TEST PREPARATION

African American History For Dummies
978-0-7645-5469-8

Algebra For Dummies
978-0-7645-5325-7

Algebra Workbook For Dummies
978-0-7645-8467-1

Art History For Dummies
978-0-470-09910-0

ASVAB For Dummies, 2nd Edition
978-0-470-10671-6

British Military History For Dummies
978-0-470-03213-8

Calculus For Dummies
978-0-7645-2498-1

Canadian History For Dummies, 2nd Edition
978-0-470-83656-9

Geometry Workbook For Dummies
978-0-471-79940-5

The SAT I For Dummies, 6th Edition
978-0-7645-7193-0

Series 7 Exam For Dummies
978-0-470-09932-2

World History For Dummies
978-0-7645-5242-7

FOOD, GARDEN, HOBBIES & HOME

Bridge For Dummies, 2nd Edition
978-0-471-92426-5

Coin Collecting For Dummies, 2nd Edition
978-0-470-22275-1

Cooking Basics For Dummies, 3rd Edition
978-0-7645-7206-7

Drawing For Dummies
978-0-7645-5476-6

Etiquette For Dummies, 2nd Edition
978-0-470-10672-3

Gardening Basics For Dummies*†
978-0-470-03749-2

Knitting Patterns For Dummies
978-0-470-04556-5

Living Gluten-Free For Dummies†
978-0-471-77383-2

Painting Do-It-Yourself For Dummies
978-0-470-17533-0

HEALTH, SELF HELP, PARENTING & PETS

Anger Management For Dummies
978-0-470-03715-7

Anxiety & Depression Workbook For Dummies
978-0-7645-9793-0

Dieting For Dummies, 2nd Edition
978-0-7645-4149-0

Dog Training For Dummies, 2nd Edition
978-0-7645-8418-3

Horseback Riding For Dummies
978-0-470-09719-9

Infertility For Dummies†
978-0-470-11518-3

Meditation For Dummies with CD-ROM, 2nd Edition
978-0-471-77774-8

Post-Traumatic Stress Disorder For Dummies
978-0-470-04922-8

Puppies For Dummies, 2nd Edition
978-0-470-03717-1

Thyroid For Dummies, 2nd Edition†
978-0-471-78755-6

Type 1 Diabetes For Dummies*†
978-0-470-17811-9

---

* Separate Canadian edition also available

† Separate U.K. edition also available

Available wherever books are sold. For more information or to order direct: U.S. customers visit www.dummies.com or call 1-877-762-2974.
U.K. customers visit www.wileyeurope.com or call (0) 1243 843291. Canadian customers visit www.wiley.ca or call 1-800-567-4797.

INTERNET & DIGITAL MEDIA

AdWords For Dummies
978-0-470-15252-2

Blogging For Dummies, 2nd Edition
978-0-470-23017-6

Digital Photography All-in-One Desk Reference For Dummies, 3rd Edition
978-0-470-03743-0

Digital Photography For Dummies, 5th Edition
978-0-7645-9802-9

Digital SLR Cameras & Photography For Dummies, 2nd Edition
978-0-470-14927-0

eBay Business All-in-One Desk Reference For Dummies
978-0-7645-8438-1

eBay For Dummies, 5th Edition*
978-0-470-04529-9

eBay Listings That Sell For Dummies
978-0-471-78912-3

Facebook For Dummies
978-0-470-26273-3

The Internet For Dummies, 11th Edition
978-0-470-12174-0

Investing Online For Dummies, 5th Edition
978-0-7645-8456-5

iPod & iTunes For Dummies, 5th Edition
978-0-470-17474-6

MySpace For Dummies
978-0-470-09529-4

Podcasting For Dummies
978-0-471-74898-4

Search Engine Optimization For Dummies, 2nd Edition
978-0-471-97998-2

Second Life For Dummies
978-0-470-18025-9

Starting an eBay Business For Dummies, 3rd Edition†
978-0-470-14924-9

GRAPHICS, DESIGN & WEB DEVELOPMENT

Adobe Creative Suite 3 Design Premium All-in-One Desk Reference For Dummies
978-0-470-11724-8

Adobe Web Suite CS3 All-in-One Desk Reference For Dummies
978-0-470-12099-6

AutoCAD 2008 For Dummies
978-0-470-11650-0

Building a Web Site For Dummies, 3rd Edition
978-0-470-14928-7

Creating Web Pages All-in-One Desk Reference For Dummies, 3rd Edition
978-0-470-09629-1

Creating Web Pages For Dummies, 8th Edition
978-0-470-08030-6

Dreamweaver CS3 For Dummies
978-0-470-11490-2

Flash CS3 For Dummies
978-0-470-12100-9

Google SketchUp For Dummies
978-0-470-13744-4

InDesign CS3 For Dummies
978-0-470-11865-8

Photoshop CS3 All-in-One Desk Reference For Dummies
978-0-470-11195-6

Photoshop CS3 For Dummies
978-0-470-11193-2

Photoshop Elements 5 For Dummies
978-0-470-09810-3

SolidWorks For Dummies
978-0-7645-9555-4

Visio 2007 For Dummies
978-0-470-08983-5

Web Design For Dummies, 2nd Edition
978-0-471-78117-2

Web Sites Do-It-Yourself For Dummies
978-0-470-16903-2

Web Stores Do-It-Yourself For Dummies
978-0-470-17443-2

LANGUAGES, RELIGION & SPIRITUALITY

Arabic For Dummies
978-0-471-77270-5

Chinese For Dummies, Audio Set
978-0-470-12766-7

French For Dummies
978-0-7645-5193-2

German For Dummies
978-0-7645-5195-6

Hebrew For Dummies
978-0-7645-5489-6

Ingles Para Dummies
978-0-7645-5427-8

Italian For Dummies, Audio Set
978-0-470-09586-7

Italian Verbs For Dummies
978-0-471-77389-4

Japanese For Dummies
978-0-7645-5429-2

Latin For Dummies
978-0-7645-5431-5

Portuguese For Dummies
978-0-471-78738-9

Russian For Dummies
978-0-471-78001-4

Spanish Phrases For Dummies
978-0-7645-7204-3

Spanish For Dummies
978-0-7645-5194-9

Spanish For Dummies, Audio Set
978-0-470-09585-0

The Bible For Dummies
978-0-7645-5296-0

Catholicism For Dummies
978-0-7645-5391-2

The Historical Jesus For Dummies
978-0-470-16785-4

Islam For Dummies
978-0-7645-5503-9

Spirituality For Dummies, 2nd Edition
978-0-470-19142-2

NETWORKING AND PROGRAMMING

ASP.NET 3.5 For Dummies
978-0-470-19592-5

C# 2008 For Dummies
978-0-470-19109-5

Hacking For Dummies, 2nd Edition
978-0-470-05235-8

Home Networking For Dummies, 4th Edition
978-0-470-11806-1

Java For Dummies, 4th Edition
978-0-470-08716-9

Microsoft® SQL Server™ 2008 All-in-One Desk Reference For Dummies
978-0-470-17954-3

Networking All-in-One Desk Reference For Dummies, 2nd Edition
978-0-7645-9939-2

Networking For Dummies, 8th Edition
978-0-470-05620-2

SharePoint 2007 For Dummies
978-0-470-09941-4

Wireless Home Networking For Dummies, 2nd Edition
978-0-471-74940-0

OPERATING SYSTEMS & COMPUTER BASICS

iMac For Dummies, 5th Edition
978-0-7645-8458-9

Laptops For Dummies, 2nd Edition
978-0-470-05432-1

Linux For Dummies, 8th Edition
978-0-470-11649-4

MacBook For Dummies
978-0-470-04859-7

**Mac OS X Leopard All-in-One
Desk Reference For Dummies**
978-0-470-05434-5

Mac OS X Leopard For Dummies
978-0-470-05433-8

Macs For Dummies, 9th Edition
978-0-470-04849-8

PCs For Dummies, 11th Edition
978-0-470-13728-4

Windows® Home Server For Dummies
978-0-470-18592-6

Windows Server 2008 For Dummies
978-0-470-18043-3

**Windows Vista All-in-One
Desk Reference For Dummies**
978-0-471-74941-7

Windows Vista For Dummies
978-0-471-75421-3

Windows Vista Security For Dummies
978-0-470-11805-4

SPORTS, FITNESS & MUSIC

Coaching Hockey For Dummies
978-0-470-83685-9

Coaching Soccer For Dummies
978-0-471-77381-8

Fitness For Dummies, 3rd Edition
978-0-7645-7851-9

Football For Dummies, 3rd Edition
978-0-470-12536-6

GarageBand For Dummies
978-0-7645-7323-1

Golf For Dummies, 3rd Edition
978-0-471-76871-5

Guitar For Dummies, 2nd Edition
978-0-7645-9904-0

**Home Recording For Musicians
For Dummies, 2nd Edition**
978-0-7645-8884-6

**iPod & iTunes For Dummies,
5th Edition**
978-0-470-17474-6

Music Theory For Dummies
978-0-7645-7838-0

Stretching For Dummies
978-0-470-06741-3

Get smart @ dummies.com®

- **Find a full list of Dummies titles**
- **Look into loads of FREE on-site articles**
- **Sign up for FREE eTips e-mailed to you weekly**
- **See what other products carry the Dummies name**
- **Shop directly from the Dummies bookstore**
- **Enter to win new prizes every month!**

* Separate Canadian edition also available
† Separate U.K. edition also available

Available wherever books are sold. For more information or to order direct: U.S. customers visit www.dummies.com or call 1-877-762-2974.
U.K. customers visit www.wileyeurope.com or call (0) 1243 843291. Canadian customers visit www.wiley.ca or call 1-800-567-4797.

APR   2011

MMA Weight Classes for Men

Class	Weight Range
Flyweight	Up to 105 lbs
Super flyweight	105.1–115 lbs
Bantamweight	115.1–125 lbs
Super bantamweight	125.1–135 lbs
Featherweight	135.1–145 lbs
Lightweight	145.1–155 lbs
Super lightweight	155.1–165 lbs
Welterweight	165.1–175 lbs
Super welterweight	175.1–185 lbs
Middleweight	185.1–195 lbs
Super middleweight	195.1–205 lbs
Light heavyweight	205.1–225 lbs
Heavyweight	225.1–265 lbs
Super heavyweight	Over 265 lbs

MMA Weight Classes for Women

Class	Weight Range
Flyweight	Up to 95 lbs
Bantamweight	95.1–105 lbs
Featherweight	105.1–115 lbs
Lightweight	115.1–125 lbs
Welterweight	125.1–135 lbs
Middleweight	135.1–145 lbs
Light heavyweight	145.1–155 lbs
Cruiserweight	155.1–165 lbs
Heavyweight	165.1–185 lbs
Super heavyweight	Over 185 lbs

MMA Fight Prohibitions

The following actions aren't allowed during an MMA fight:

- No groin attacks.
- No knees to the head on a grounded opponent.
- No strikes to the back of the head or the spine.
- No head butts.
- No eye gouging.
- No fish hooking.
- No fingers in an opponent's orifices.
- No biting.
- No hair pulling.
- No strikes or grabbing of the throat.
- No manipulation of the fingers or toes.
- No intentional grabbing of the ring or cage.
- No intentional throwing of your opponent outside of the ring or cage.

MMA Gear

Here are the items you need to practice MMA:

- **MMA gloves:** Necessary for competitions. Wear them during sparring and grappling sessions as well so you can get accustomed to them.
- **Boxing gloves:** Essential for working on strikes.
- **Handwraps:** Good for protecting your hands when training or fighting competitively.
- **Headgear:** Used for sparring to protect the skull from harsh blows.
- **Cup:** Essential for male MMA fighters.
- **Mouthpiece:** Essential for protecting your teeth while competing and training. Try conditioning while wearing a mouthpiece to get used to wearing one.
- **MMA shin guards:** Helpful for protecting your shins when training or sparring.
- **Stability ball:** A great tool for working on your balance and control.
- **Jump rope:** Useful for warming up before training and a common tool for MMA practitioners.
- **Thai pads and focus mitts:** Good for using with a partner when you want to work on knees, kicks, and other strikes.
- **Kettlebells:** One of my favorite tools for full-body conditioning.
- **MMA attire:** Can be worn inside and outside of the ring and includes T-shirts, hoodies, sweats, and shorts.

Nutritional Advice

If you want to maintain your weight *and* nourish your body while in training mode, do the following:

- **Eat at least five meals a day.** Each meal should be the size of your clenched fist and contain vegetables and complex carbohydrates from live sources. I'm a fan of oatmeal, bran, corn, yams, carrots, potatoes, beans, and lentils.
- **Drink lots and lots of water.** Keeping yourself hydrated is essential every day, not just when you're training. So get in the habit of drinking a gallon of water per day.
- **Don't let supplements and protein shakes stand in for a good diet.** Yes, supplements and shakes are a good way to get essential nutrients, but the best way to score key nutrients for your body is to get them from live sources. Build a good habit of eating healthy food and only use vitamins, supplements, and shakes to *add* to your already healthy diet.

If you need to lose or gain weight before a fight, work out a plan with your trainer.

Copyright © 2009 Wiley Publishing, Inc. All rights reserved. Item 9017-9.
For more information about Wiley Publishing, call 1-800-762-2974.

For Dummies: Bestselling Book Series for Beginners

FROZEN PALEO

DAIRY-FREE ICE CREAM, POPS, PIES, GRANITAS, SORBETS, AND MORE

PAMELA BRAUN

The Countryman Press
A division of W. W. Norton & Company
Independent Publishers Since 1923

For information about permission to reproduce selections from this book, write to
Permissions, The Countryman Press, 500 Fifth Avenue, New York, NY 10110

For information about special discounts for bulk purchases, please contact
W. W. Norton Special Sales at specialsales@wwnorton.com or 800-233-4830

The Countryman Press
www.countrymanpress.com
A division of W. W. Norton & Company, Inc.
500 Fifth Avenue, New York, NY 10110
www.wwnorton.com

978-1-58157-386-2 (pbk.)

10 9 8 7 6 5 4 3 2 1

CONTENTS

BANANA CREAM PIE 84

CHOCOLATE CREAM PIE 89

HEATHER'S MOCHA ALMOND FUDGE PIE 92

BAKED ALASKA 97

AFFOGATO 102

HOT CHOCOLATE WITH ICE CREAM 105

ICY FROZEN TREATS

STRAWBERRY SORBET 111

LEMON SORBET 112

CUCUMBER PINEAPPLE SORBET 115

PEACHES AND CREAM SORBET 116

ORANGE SORBET 119

HONEY PEACH SORBET 122

ISLAND PARADISE SORBET 125

INTRODUCTION

Following the Paleo way of eating doesn't mean you can't indulge your sweet tooth once in a while. But is it possible to actually have a delicious frozen treat that's also Paleo? I'm here to tell you it is.

I've been lactose intolerant for years and have been making dairy-free ice creams for a long time. These frozen treats will satisfy any sweets craving, and keep you on the Paleo path guilt-free.

Making your own ice cream is fun and rewarding. What's the reward, you ask? A delicious bowl of ice cream that only contains the ingredients you put into it. No additives or preservatives and ingredients you can't pronounce.

If you're thinking that Paleo frozen treats have got to be thin and icy—because they're missing the fat from all that dairy cream that goes into making normal ice cream—I can assure you that's not the case. In many of these recipes you'll use full-fat coconut cream to replace the dairy cream. The fact that 1 tablespoon of coconut cream contains 5.20 grams of fat (USDA)* and a tablespoon of dairy heavy cream contains 5.41 (USDA)** grams of fat means you won't be missing that yummy creaminess that you're looking for in a frozen treat.

And it's not just coconut cream in these recipes. You'll also find full-fat coconut milk (the stuff in the can . . . not from the carton in the dairy department of your grocery store) and cashew cream. These ingredients ensure the creaminess of your homemade ice cream. While there are other nut creams available, I use cashew cream in these recipes because it's creamier and has a more neutral flavor than other nut creams.

---

* http://ndb.nal.usda.gov/ndb/foods/show/3661

** http://ndb.nal.usda.gov/ndb/foods/show/52

Something you're going to notice when you make your own ice cream is that it will be *really* hard when you pull it out of the freezer. Don't worry, you didn't mess anything up—that's just what happens with homemade ice cream. You can let it sit out for about twenty minutes or pop it in the microwave for a few seconds before digging your spoon into it. There are a couple of reasons that this happens: one is that your home ice cream maker doesn't whip in as much air into the ice cream as the commercial ice cream makers do. Another reason is that homemade ice cream doesn't have all the additives that most commercial ice creams have, which are added to make them softer. I think this last one is a really good trade-off—knowing exactly what's in the ice cream you'll be eating is worth a few extra moments of waiting.

INGREDIENTS

I recommend organic ingredients for these recipes. I also highly recommend buying the highest quality ingredients you can afford. There are so few ingredients in many of these recipes that you will taste everything that's in the ice cream, so you want the best you can get.

We've already discussed the base ingredients for the ice cream (coconut cream, coconut milk, and cashew cream) but what about the sweeteners and flavors?

PURE MAPLE SYRUP — Make sure that the syrup you are buying is pure maple syrup and not pancake or breakfast syrup. Pure maple syrup has only one ingredient listed: "maple syrup." Organic is even better. Pancake or breakfast syrups are made from high fructose corn syrup and flavorings to make them taste like maple. In the United States, they're not allowed to put the word "maple" on the label of these products.

Canada produces roughly 80 percent of the world's supply of maple syrup, and they have a number and letter grading system: #1 includes AA (extra light), A (light), and B (medium); #2 includes C (amber); and #3 includes D (dark).

The United States has a different grading system and only includes two letters: A or B. A is lighter tasting and is for eating straight up, like on pancakes. B is darker and is used more in baking and cooking. Grade A maple syrup is broken down by color, so you may see the terms "light amber," "medium amber," or "dark amber" on your bottle of syrup. I tend to use grade B syrup in my recipes because I like the richer flavor it gives to the ice cream, but if you can only find A, it will work the same.

PURE MAPLE SUGAR — This is made by boiling off the excess water from maple syrup. Maple sugar isn't graded, so it's not as confusing as buying the syrup can be.

PURE COCONUT SUGAR — Coconut sugar is made in much the same way as maple sugar is. The palm tree is tapped for its sap, which is then boiled until all that remains is the sugar. Coconut sugar contains higher amounts of magnesium, nitrogen, and Vitamin C than any other natural sweetener.* Because it is darker in color, it will affect the color of your finished product a little bit.

RAW HONEY — You might be asking why specifically "raw" honey as opposed to just honey in general. Well, when honey is processed, it's heated, which causes a lot of the benefits of honey to be cooked away. Raw honey has not been heated, and therefore all the good things that honey contains can still be found in the sweetener. What are these "good" things found in honey? Well, without getting into too much detail, it's been found that honey is an all-natural antibiotic, and contains pre-biotics and some antioxidants.

CASHEW CREAM — Making cashew cream is easy to do with a high speed blender. All it takes is 1 cup raw cashews, soaked in water overnight, and ½ cup water. After soaking, drain the cashews and pour them into your blender. Add the ½ cup water, cover and blend until the cashews are smooth. This shouldn't take longer than a minute or two. Use a spatula to scrape the cream from the blender and it's ready to use. Your homemade cashew cream will last a week in a covered container in your refrigerator. Just re-stir it before you use it.

CASHEW MILK — Making cashew milk is also easy to do with a high speed blender. Soak 1 cup of raw cashews in water overnight. Drain the water and toss cashews into the blender. Add 2 cups of water and run the blender until everything is creamy and there are no pieces of cashews floating around. This should take about 2 minutes.

---

* http://paleoleap.com/sugar-and-paleo

UNSWEETENED COCOA POWDER — When buying unsweetened cocoa, the only ingredient listed should be unsweetened cocoa. You don't want to buy anything that's got any fillers or weird ingredients in it. Also, the better quality cocoa you buy, the more intense the chocolate flavor will be in the finished product.

UNSWEETENED CHOCOLATE — This is the stuff that you accidentally ate as a kid, thinking you scored a super thick chocolate bar, and promptly spit it out because it wasn't sweet and tasted terrible. I use 99 percent or 100 percent chocolate, and the ingredient list on my bars says "cocoa beans." (The 99 percent chocolate bar is cocoa beans and vanilla beans.)

RAW COCOA BUTTER — You might be more familiar with cocoa butter for applying to dry skin or in the prevention of scars, but there's also an edible cocoa butter. Cocoa butter is made from cold pressing cocoa nibs to separate a cocoa paste from the powder of the nibs. You'll need to make sure you are buying the edible cocoa butter. Some stores carry it but it is readily available online.

HELPFUL THINGS TO KNOW
ABOUT DAIRY-FREE ICE CREAMS

The two most important ingredients when making any ice cream are sugar and fat. These aren't just important because of their flavor impact, but in how the ice cream freezes as well.

SUGAR

Remember earlier when I mentioned that homemade ice cream freezes harder than store-bought ice cream? Another reason for that is the amount of sugar that is used in the ice cream. The lower the sugar content (regardless of the source), the harder it freezes. It can also cause the ice cream to have an icy texture on your tongue. One way to help prevent this is by using thickeners (things like bananas or arrowroot). There are a couple of recipes in this book that use thickeners, but most do not. I like my ice cream to taste like the pure flavor that it should have, so I tend not to use thickeners. This doesn't mean that the ice creams are icy though. I have used as little sugar as I can in these recipes to help keep the recipes as Paleo friendly as they can be.

FAT

The amount of fat in an ice cream will help to determine how creamy the ice cream feels in your mouth. I talked about using coconut cream and coconut milk earlier in the book. Using the combination of both coconut milk and coconut cream works a lot like using regular dairy milk and dairy cream in the making of ice cream: it helps to keep the Paleo ice cream rich and creamy feeling on the tongue. I don't simply rely on the fat found in the coconut milk alone, as it's not enough to get that rich and creamy texture you're looking for.

TECHNIQUE

While cooking the ice cream base, it's easiest if you use a whisk to easily and thoroughly incorporate all of the ingredients. The whisk also keeps all the ingredients moving so that you don't have ingredients getting stuck on the bottom or potentially burning on the sides of the pan.

In all of my recipes, I recommend that you chill the ice cream base before pouring it into your ice cream maker. If you pour warm ice cream base into your ice cream maker it won't freeze properly, if it freezes at all. I advise laying a piece of plastic wrap on the surface of the ice cream base before putting it into the refrigerator to chill. This keeps the base from forming a skin on top while it chills. I also recommend giving the chilled ice cream base a good stir before pouring it into the ice cream freezer. This helps to mix up any ingredients that may have settled or separated before freezing.

ICE CREAM MAKER — Your specific ice cream maker will let you know how to process the ingredients into ice cream, but for freezing the ice cream I recommend a long and shallow freezer-safe container. If the container is shallow, it will thaw a bit faster when you are ready to serve it. A deep container will keep the ice cream frozen longer.

BLENDER — For the best results, I recommend a high-speed blender, like a Ninja or Vitamix. The high speed blender does a much better job of blending everything up into the smallest pieces possible. It's much better than a standard blender. This is especially true when it comes to making the cashew cream and milk.

TIPS & TRICKS TO MAKE
ICE CREAM MAKING EASIER

- A lot of these ice cream recipes use a custard base to make them rich and creamy. This calls for using egg yolks. When making the custard you should get the mixture somewhere between 160–170 degrees Fahrenheit (71–77 degrees Celsius). If cooking with egg yolks makes you uncomfortable, use eggs that are pasteurized in their shells (like Safest Choice eggs).

- Remember, this is homemade ice cream. What does that mean, aside from the fact that you know everything that has gone into making it? Well, it's going to be much harder than store-bought ice cream. It has nothing do with the ingredients—it's all about air, or the lack thereof. Store-bought ice cream is made in large machines that whip a lot of air into the ice cream mixture, and that helps to keep the ice cream soft and scoopable. You won't be able to bring out that container of vanilla ice cream and jam a spoon right into and start eating. You'll either need to pop it in the microwave (for 10 second intervals on HIGH) or let it sit on the counter for roughly 20 minutes before digging in.

- While there *are* sweeteners in these ice cream recipes, the quantities used are lower than normal and the sweeteners used are not refined sugars. As such, you may find that these recipes aren't as sweet as what you are used to, but I think you'll find they are sweet enough, and much better for you.

- The unrefined sugars that are used in these recipes may slightly alter the colors of some of the ice creams or their components. Because coconut sugar is brown, the meringue on the Baked Alaska is more beige than bright white. You'll also notice that the mango sorbet isn't quite as bright orange as the store-bought stuff. Again, that's because the coconut sugar is brown . . . not white.

- The coconut cream that is called for in these recipes is bought as coconut cream. It is *not* from the little bit of cream that you find at the top of a chilled can of coconut milk. It is also not the stuff you find in the liquor aisle at your grocery store. Coconut cream is available in cans and aseptic boxes in stores and online.

- The coconut milk that is in these recipes is full-fat coconut milk. It is *not* the stuff you find in the non-dairy section in your grocery store.

- Because every ice cream maker is different, the instructions in this book will suggest you refer to your maker's owner's manual for the actual processing of your ice cream.

- When making these recipes, make sure you use the best ingredients you can find. There are so few ingredients in these recipes that every ingredient really counts toward the end flavor of the frozen treat.

CREAMY FROZEN TREATS

~ FUZZ BUZZ ~
ICE CREAM

MAKES 1 QUART

What can make a cop stop (besides you speeding past at 90 mph)? Coffee and doughnuts, of course! This ice cream is full of Paleo doughnut chunks surrounded by a coffee ice cream that will make you stop too. Why should the police be the only ones who get to eat the fun stuff?

1. Preheat the oven to 350 degrees Fahrenheit (180 degrees Celsius).

2. Beat the eggs with the sugar and oil until they are well blended and smooth.

3. Add the milk, vanilla, cider vinegar, and salt to the mixture and continue beating.

4. Finally, stir in the coconut flour and baking soda and mix until thoroughly blended.

5. Fill 8 lined muffin tins with dough (from a circle doughnut pan) or 6 well-greased donut circles.

6. Bake for 20 minutes or until a toothpick inserted into the center of the muffin/doughnut comes out clean.

7. Set doughnuts aside to cool.

FOR THE DOUGHNUTS

3 large whole eggs

¼ cup coconut palm sugar (50g)

¼ cup coconut oil (60ml)

½ cup full-fat coconut milk (120ml)

1 teaspoon pure vanilla extract (5ml)

1 teaspoon cider vinegar (5ml)

¼ teaspoon sea salt

½ cup coconut flour (64g)

½ teaspoon baking soda

1 (13.5 ounce) can full-fat
  coconut milk (400ml)

1¾ cups full-fat coconut cream
  (420ml)

¼ cup raw honey (60ml)

½ cup brewed black coffee
  (120ml)

4 teaspoons instant espresso
  powder (8g)

6 large egg yolks

Pinch of sea salt

8. Whisk all of the ice cream ingredients together in a 4-quart pot.

9. Cook over medium heat and bring to just a simmer (about 10 to 15 minutes). While this is cooking you will need to be whisking it from time to time to keep things from sticking to the sides and bottom of the pan.

10. Since you're making a custard, you want it to be between 160 to 170 degrees Fahrenheit (71 to 77 degrees Celsius). To see if your custard is done, simply dip a spoon into the mixture and run your finger down the back of the spoon. If the line stays clean, your custard is done. If the line blurs again, you need a little more time to make the custard.

11. Remove the pot from the heat and let it cool for at least 30 minutes. Pour the mixture into a refrigerator-safe container and cover with plastic wrap, making sure the plastic wrap is covering the top of the liquid (this keeps a skin from forming on top of your custard). Place this into the refrigerator and chill for at least 6 hours. Chilling overnight is best.

12. If the custard separates while cooling, simply stir it before pouring it into the ice cream maker.

13. Pour the chilled mixture into an ice cream maker and process according to the manufacturer's instructions. During the last 2 to 3 minutes of processing, tear the doughnuts into 1 inch (2.5 centimeter) pieces and drop them into the ice cream. This will ensure they are well-mixed into the ice cream.

14. Transfer the mixture to an airtight, freezer-safe container and freeze for 2 to 3 hours before serving.

~ SALTED CARAMEL ~
STRACCIATELLA
ICE CREAM

MAKES 1 QUART

There's salted caramel and then there's stracciatella ice cream, but what happens when you put the two together? It's like a cosmic explosion of the very good kind. This rich and creamy caramel ice cream has a salty hint to it that gets tamed by all those billions of tiny chocolate shreds floating in the ice cream. When I make this I CAN'T STOP EATING IT.

FOR THE CARAMEL

1 cup maple syrup (240ml)
¼ cup water (60ml)
1 (13.5 ounce) can full-fat coconut milk (400ml)

FOR THE ICE CREAM

1¼ cups full-fat coconut cream (300ml)
1 teaspoon sea salt
3 large egg yolks
1 teaspoon pure vanilla bean paste (5ml)

1. To make the caramel, add the maple syrup and water to a 4- or 5-quart pot and bring to a boil over medium high heat. Cover the pan for 2 minutes (this keeps the sugar crystals from forming on the sides of the pan).

2. Remove the cover and keep cooking and swirling the pan until you get a deep amber color (the bubbles will change color too).

3. Add coconut milk to the mixture, then whisk it and take off the heat (the mixture may bubble quite violently when you add the coconut milk; just keep whisking until it goes down). Set the pan aside.

4. In another large pan whisk the coconut cream, salt, and egg yolks together. Heat over medium high heat until mixture is hot (about 5 to 7 minutes). Do not bring this to a boil.

¼ cup unsweetened cocoa
  powder (21g)

5 tablespoons coconut oil
  (75ml)

2 teaspoons maple syrup (13g)

5. Pour the coconut cream mixture into the caramel mixture and bring the whole thing to a boil, over medium-high heat, for 20 seconds.

6. Remove the pot from heat and pour the mixture into a bowl; stir in the vanilla bean paste and extra salt (if you like your caramel salty). Let the mixture cool for at least one hour, then cover with plastic wrap and make sure that plastic wrap is covering the top of the liquid (this keeps a skin from forming on top of your custard). Place this into the refrigerator and chill for at least 6 hours. Chilling overnight is best.

7. Before churning the ice cream (according to manufacturer's instructions), we'll mix up the chocolate. Add the cocoa powder, coconut oil, and maple syrup together in a small bowl and stir to thoroughly combine. Set the mixture aside.

8. Churn the ice cream according to manufacturer's instructions. During the last 2 to 3 minutes of churning, slowly drizzle ⅔ of the chocolate mixture into ice cream. Do this slowly so that the chocolate breaks up into tiny pieces.

9. Scoop the ice cream into a freezer-safe bowl and smooth out the top. Now spread the remaining chocolate mixture on top of the ice cream. Cover and place in the freezer for 2 to 3 hours before serving.

~ PURE VANILLA ~
ICE CREAM

MAKES 1 QUART

What more can be said about pure vanilla ice cream. It's the real deal! The vanilla flavor in this luscious ice cream is intense and the vanilla flecks are abundant.

1 (13.5-ounce) can full-fat coconut milk (400ml)

1 ¾ cups full-fat coconut cream (420ml)

¼ cup maple syrup (60ml)

4 large egg yolks

Pinch of sea salt

1 tablespoon pure vanilla bean paste (15g)

1. Whisk all of the ice cream ingredients together in a 4-quart pot.

2. Cook the mixture over medium heat and bring to just a simmer (about 10 to 15 minutes). While this is cooking you will need to whisk it from time to time to keep the mixture from sticking to the sides and bottom of the pan.

3. Since you're making a custard, you want it to be between 160 to 170 degrees Fahrenheit (71 to 77 degrees Celsius). To see if your custard is done, simply dip a spoon into the mixture and run your finger down the back of the spoon. If the line stays clean, your custard is done. If the line blurs again, you need a little more time to make the custard.

4. Remove the pot from the heat and let it cool for at least 30 minutes. Pour the mixture into a refrigerator-safe container and cover with plastic wrap, making sure the plastic wrap is covering the top of the liquid (this keeps a skin from forming on

top of your custard). Place this into the refrigerator and chill for at least 6 hours. Chilling overnight is best.

5. If the custard separates while cooling, simply stir it before pouring it into the ice cream maker.

6. Pour the chilled mixture into an ice cream maker and process according to the manufacturer's instructions.

7. Transfer to an airtight, freezer-safe container and freeze for 2 to 3 hours before serving.

~ MAPLE WALNUT ~
ICE CREAM

MAKES 1 PINT

Maple walnut ice cream was once a very popular flavor in the ice cream aisle. It has since fallen down the ladder of flavor favorites, probably due to all the ice creams that have bits and chunks of everything in them, and I think that's just sad. Maple walnut isn't only an autumn flavor either: the sweetness of maple combined with the earthy flavor of walnuts is something for which your palate will call out. Trust me on this, you're going to love it.

1. Toast the walnuts in a large frying pan over medium heat, just until they begin to smell nutty (about 3 minutes).

2. Finely chop ½ cup nuts and set them aside until the end.

3. Bring the cashew and coconut creams to a simmer in a heavy-bottomed pot. Remove the mixture from the heat and add the finely chopped walnuts. Stir, cover the pan, and let the nuts steep for 2 hours.

4. Whisk the egg yolks, maple syrup, and salt together in a heavy-bottomed pan. Strain the walnut mixture into the egg mixture (throw out the nuts).

Ingredients
1 cup walnuts (128g), divided
1 cup cashew cream (240ml)
1 (13.5 ounce) can full-fat coconut cream (400ml)
4 large egg yolks
½ cup maple syrup (120ml)
½ teaspoon sea salt

5. Since you're making a custard, you want it to be between 160 to 170 degrees Fahrenheit (71 to 77 degrees Celsius). To see if your custard is done, simply dip a spoon into the mixture and run your finger down the back of the spoon. If the line stays clean, your custard is done. If the line blurs again, you need a little more time to make the custard.

6. Remove the pot from the heat and let it cool for at least 30 minutes. Pour the mixture into a refrigerator-safe container and cover with plastic wrap, making sure the plastic wrap is covering the top of the liquid (this keeps a skin from forming on top of your custard). Place this into the refrigerator and chill for at least 6 hours. Chilling overnight is best.

7. If the custard separates while cooling, simply stir it before pouring it into the ice cream maker.

8. Begin churning the ice cream according to the manufacturer's instructions. While the ice cream is churning, roughly chop the remaining walnuts.

9. Add the walnuts to the ice cream during the last minute of churning.

10. Scoop the ice cream into a lidded container and freeze for 3 to 4 hours before serving.

~ DREAMY BITES ~
ICE CREAM

MAKES 24 BITES

Sometimes you want just a little bit of ice cream, but know you just won't be able to stop from finishing the whole container. That's why there are ice cream bites! These small, dreamy bites will give you that "little bit" of ice cream you're looking for with the added bonus of some crispy, crunchy chocolate coating on the outside.

1. Whisk all of the ice cream ingredients together in a 4-quart pot.

2. Cook the ingredients over medium heat and bring to just a simmer (about 10 to 15 minutes). Whisk this continually while cooking to prevent the ingredients from sticking to the sides and bottom of the pan.

3. Since you're making a custard, you want it to be between 160 to 170 degrees Fahrenheit (71 to 77 degrees Celsius). To see if your custard is done, simply dip a spoon into the mixture and run your finger down the back of the spoon. If the line stays clean, your custard is done. If the line blurs again, you need a little more time to make the custard.

FOR THE VANILLA ICE CREAM

1 (13.5-ounce) can full-fat coconut milk (400ml)

1¾ cups coconut cream (420ml)

¼ cup maple syrup (60ml)

4 egg yolks

1 tablespoon vanilla bean paste (15g)

Pinch of sea salt

4. Remove the pot from the heat and let it cool for at least 30 minutes. Pour the mixture into a refrigerator-safe container and cover with plastic wrap, making sure the plastic wrap is covering the top of the liquid (this keeps a skin from forming on top of your custard). Place this into the refrigerator and chill for at least 6 hours. Chilling overnight is best.

5. If the custard separates while cooling, simply stir it before pouring it into the ice cream maker.

6. Pour the chilled mixture into an ice cream maker and process according to the manufacturer's instructions.

7. Freeze for 2 to 3 hours.

8. Mix the chocolate coating ingredients together and whisk until they are thoroughly combined. It's easier to dip the bites if you put the chocolate mixture into a narrow and deep bowl.

9. Line a baking sheet with parchment paper.

10. Use a small ice cream scoop to scoop out the ice cream. Use the palm of your hand to really push the ice cream into the scoop so that you get a nice shape.

11. Pop the ice cream from the scoop out onto the parchment lined baking sheet and continue the process with all of the ice cream.

FOR THE CHOCOLATE COATING

½ cup unsweetened cocoa powder (42g)

10 tablespoons coconut oil (150ml)

4 teaspoons maple syrup (15ml)

12. Place the baking sheet back into the freezer for two hours.

13. After two hours, remove the baking sheet from the freezer. You're now ready to dip your dreamy bites.

14. Rest an ice cream bite on the tines of a fork and drop it into the chocolate coating. Turn the bite so that it's completely covered.

15. Scoop the bite out of the chocolate with the fork and gently slide it back onto the parchment lined baking sheet. You may need a second fork to help get the coated bite off the first fork (they sometimes tend to stick as the coating freezes).

16. Continue this process for the rest of the bites.

17. Pop the baking sheet back into the freezer for one hour before enjoying.

VANILLA ~ CARAMEL ~ SWIRL ICE CREAM

MAKES 1 QUART

What's not to love about anything that's caramel swirled? Well, this flavor is going to be a big hit. The caramel is rich and creamy and you won't believe how little sugar it has once you've had a bite. Mix that with vanilla ice cream and how could you go wrong?

FOR THE CARAMEL

4 tablespoons ghee (60ml)

2 tablespoons water (30g)

½ cup coconut palm sugar (81g)

½ cup full-fat coconut milk (120ml)

½ teaspoon pure vanilla extract

Pinch of sea salt

1. Add ghee, water, and coconut palm sugar to a heavy-bottomed pan.

2. Heat the mixture over medium heat and continuously stir until it comes to a boil. Let it boil for two minutes.

3. Slowly pour in the coconut milk, vanilla extract, and sea salt, and stir to combine (it may hiss and pop as you add the milk). Keep whisking as you add the ingredients.

4. Cook for another 5 minutes as it thickens and make sure to periodically stir it to keep things from sticking and burning.

5. Remove the mixture from the heat and let cool.

1 (13.5-ounce) can full-fat
coconut milk (400ml)

1¾ cups coconut cream
(420ml)

¼ cup maple syrup (60ml)

4 egg yolks

1 tablespoon vanilla bean paste
(15g)

Pinch of sea salt

6. Whisk all of the ice cream ingredients together in a 4-quart pot.

7. Cook the mixture over medium heat and bring to just a simmer (about 10 to 15 minutes). Whisk this continually while cooking to prevent the ingredients from sticking to the sides and bottom of the pan.

8. Since you're making a custard, you want it to be between 160 to 170 degrees Fahrenheit (71 to 77 degrees Celsius). To see if your custard is done, simply dip a spoon into the mixture and run your finger down the back of the spoon. If the line stays clean, your custard is done. If the line blurs again, you need a little more time to make the custard.

9. Remove the pot from the heat and let it cool for at least 30 minutes. Pour the mixture into a refrigerator-safe container and cover with plastic wrap, making sure the plastic wrap is covering the top of the liquid (this keeps a skin from forming on top of your custard). Place this into the refrigerator and chill for at least 6 hours. Chilling overnight is best.

10. If the custard separates while cooling, simply stir it before pouring it into the ice cream maker.

11. Pour the chilled mixture into an ice cream maker and process according to the manufacturer's instructions.

12. Scoop the ice cream into a freezer-safe container and pour the caramel on top of the ice cream. Run a knife through the caramel and ice cream to swirl them together.

13. Freeze for 2 to 3 hours before serving.

~ NUT 'N HONEY ~
ICE CREAM

There's a very popular breakfast cereal that has this flavor combination, and I just couldn't help but re-create it in a bowl of ice cream. I mean, why not start your day with dessert? This "nut'n honey" flavor would get your day started out on just the right note.

FOR THE CARAMEL

¼ cup raw honey (60ml)

¼ cup ghee (60ml)

⅝ cup coconut palm sugar (121g)

½ cup full-fat coconut cream (120ml)

FOR THE ICE CREAM

1 cup cashew cream (240ml)

1 (13.5-ounce) can full-fat coconut milk (400ml)

1 cup slivered almonds (240ml)

4 large egg yolks

½ cup raw honey (120ml)

½ teaspoon sea salt

½ cup toasted and chopped almonds (120ml)

1. To make the caramel, add the honey, ghee and coconut palm sugar to a heavy-bottomed pot and bring to a simmer over medium high heat.

2. Keep cooking and swirling the pan until the honey changes to an amber color (the bubbles will change color too).

3. Add the coconut cream to the mixture, then whisk and take it off the heat (the mixture may bubble quite violently when you add the coconut cream; just whisk until it settles down). Set the pan aside.

4. Bring the cashew cream and coconut milk to a simmer in a heavy-bottomed pot. Remove the pot from the heat and add the slivered almonds to the mixture. Stir, cover the pot, and let the nuts steep for 2 hours.

5. Whisk the egg yolks, honey, and salt together in a heavy-bottomed pan. Strain the almond mixture into the egg mixture (throw out the nuts). Cook over medium heat and bring to just a simmer

(about 10 to 15 minutes). While this is cooking you will need to whisk it from time to time to keep the mixture from sticking to the sides and bottom of the pan.

6. Since you're making a custard, you want it to be between 160 to 170 degrees Fahrenheit (71 to 77 degrees Celsius). To see if your custard is done, simply dip a spoon into the mixture and run your finger down the back of the spoon. If the line stays clean, your custard is done. If the line blurs again, you need a little more time to make the custard.

7. Remove the pot from the heat and let it cool for at least 30 minutes. Pour the mixture into a refrigerator-safe container and cover with plastic wrap, making sure the plastic wrap is covering the top of the liquid (this keeps a skin from forming on top of your custard). Place this into the refrigerator and chill for at least 6 hours. Chilling overnight is best.

8. If the custard separates while cooling, simply stir it before pouring it into the ice cream maker.

9. Begin churning the ice cream according to manufacturer's instructions. While the ice cream is churning, roughly chop the remaining almonds. Add the remaining toasted and chopped almonds to the ice cream during the last minute of churning.

10. Scoop half of the ice cream into a lidded container and then drizzle half of the caramel on top of the ice cream. Finish filling the container with the remaining ice cream and freeze for 3 to 4 hours before serving.

11. Use the rest of the caramel to drizzle over top when serving.

~ BACIO ~
ICE CREAM

MAKES 1 QUART

Who doesn't love the combination of hazelnuts and chocolate? This ice cream embodies both of those flavors so well you'll fall in love. The rich, creamy hazelnut ice cream has a swirl of chocolate running through it, so you get both of those great flavors together. This chocolate swirl recipe also makes for a fantastic-tasting chocolate sauce to pour over some of the other ice creams in this book, so this recipe is a two-fer.

1. Preheat the oven to 300 degrees Fahrenheit (148 degrees Celsius).

2. Arrange the nuts in a single layer on a rimmed baking sheet, and roast for 10 minutes. Remove the nuts from oven and place them onto a tea towel (no terrycloth towels). Fold the ends of the towel over the nuts and rub until the skins peel off.

3. Roughly chop the nuts and set ½ cup aside.

4. Bring the coconut milk and coconut cream to a simmer in a heavy-bottomed pot. Remove the pot from heat and add 1 cup of the chopped hazelnuts to the mixture. Stir, cover the pan, and let the nuts steep for 2 hours.

FOR THE ICE CREAM

1½ cups hazelnuts (213g), divided

1 (13.5-ounce can) full-fat coconut milk (400ml)

1¾ cups full-fat coconut cream (415ml)

4 large egg yolks

¼ cup + 2 tablespoons raw honey (127g)

1½ tablespoons pure vanilla bean paste (22g)

¼ teaspoon sea salt

5. Whisk the egg yolks, honey, vanilla paste, and salt together in a 4-quart heavy-bottomed pan. Strain the hazelnut mixture into the egg mixture (throw out the nuts). Cook the mixture over medium heat and bring to just a simmer (about 10 to 15 minutes). While this is cooking you will need to whisk it to keep the mixture from sticking to the sides and bottom of the pan.

6. Since you're making a custard, you want it to be between 160 to 170 degrees Fahrenheit (71 to 77 degrees Celsius). To see if your custard is done, simply dip a spoon into the mixture and run your finger down the back of the spoon. If the line stays clean, your custard is done. If the line blurs again, you need a little more time to make the custard.

7. Remove the pot from the heat and let it cool for at least 30 minutes. Pour the mixture into a refrigerator-safe container and cover with plastic wrap, making sure the plastic wrap is covering the top of the liquid (this keeps a skin from forming on top of your custard). Place this into the refrigerator and chill for at least 6 hours. Chilling overnight is best.

8. If the custard separates while cooling, simply stir it before pouring it into the ice cream maker.

9. Finely chop the chocolate and add it to the coconut milk, honey, and salt in a small bowl.

10. Microwave the mixture on high for 30-second increments. Stir between each heating and only continue to heat until the chocolate has melted. Then set the chocolate mixture aside.

11. Begin churning the ice cream according to the manufacturer's instructions. Add the remaining ½ cup hazelnuts to the ice cream during the last minute of churning.

12. Scoop half of the ice cream into a lidded container then pour the chocolate mixture on top. Spoon the remaining ice cream on top of the chocolate and freeze for 3 to 4 hours before serving.

FOR THE CHOCOLATE SWIRL

1¾ ounces unsweetened baker's chocolate (49.6g)

½ cup full-fat coconut milk (120ml)

3 tablespoons raw honey (45ml)

Pinch of sea salt

~ PISTACHIO ~
ICE CREAM
MAKES 1 PINT

Pistachio is also one of my favorite flavors of ice cream. When I was in Italy, I ate pistachio gelato every day. Thankfully we walked a lot, so my clothes still fit me at the end of the trip. This pistachio ice cream is loaded with nuts. The one big difference you will notice is that it's not bright green. To begin with, I don't use any artificial colors in my ice creams; second, I didn't use the expensive Bronte pistachio paste to make this. I wanted to be able to make an ice cream that didn't require you to search high and low for the ingredients and then pay a king's ransom to get them. This recipe is made with ingredients you can get from your local grocery store, and it tastes fantastic.

1½ cups raw pistachios (200g), divided

1 cup cashew cream (285g)

1 (13.5-ounce) can full-fat coconut milk (400ml)

4 large egg yolks

½ cup maple syrup (156g)

½ teaspoon sea salt

1. Preheat oven to 300 degrees Fahrenheit (148 degrees Celsius).

2. Arrange the pistachios on a baking sheet in a single layer and bake for 10 minutes, or until nuts begin to turn golden and smell nutty.

3. Remove the nuts from the oven and let them cool, then finely chop 1 cup nuts and set them aside.

4. Bring the cashew cream and coconut milk to a simmer in a heavy-bottomed pot. Remove the mixture from the heat and add the finely chopped pistachios. Stir, cover the pan, and let the nuts steep for 2 hours.

5. Whisk the egg yolks, maple syrup, and salt together in a 4-quart heavy-bottomed pan. Strain the pistachio mixture into the egg mixture (throw out the nuts). Cook over medium heat and bring to just a simmer (about 10 to 15 minutes). While this is cooking you will need to whisk it to keep the mixture from sticking to the sides and bottom of the pan.

6. Since you're making a custard, you want it to be between 160 to 170 degrees Fahrenheit (71 to 77 degrees Celsius). To see if your custard is done, simply dip a spoon into the mixture and run your finger down the back of the spoon. If the line stays clean, your custard is done. If the line blurs again, you need a little more time to make the custard.

7. Remove the pot from the heat and let it cool for at least 30 minutes. Pour the mixture into a refrigerator-safe container and cover with plastic wrap, making sure the plastic wrap is covering the top of the liquid (this keeps a skin from forming on top of your custard). Place this in the refrigerator and chill for at least 6 hours. Chilling overnight is best.

8. If the custard separates while cooling, simply stir it before pouring it into the ice cream maker.

9. Begin churning the ice cream according to the manufacturer's instructions. While the ice cream is churning, roughly chop remaining pistachios.

10. Add the remaining pistachios to the ice cream during the last minute of churning.

11. Scoop the ice cream into a lidded container and freeze for 3 to 4 hours before serving.

CUCKOO FOR COCONUT
ICE CREAM

MAKES 1 QUART

If you like coconut, you're going to love Cuckoo for Coconut. I'm cuckoo for the stuff, so I worked really hard to get as much coconut flavor in here as I could. For something extra delicious, try sprinkling the top of the ice cream with some Paleo chocolate chips. Good luck not eating the whole batch yourself in one sitting.

1. Preheat the oven to 300 degrees Fahrenheit (148 degrees Celsius).

2. Arrange the coconut flakes in a single layer on a baking sheet. Bake for 5 minutes or until the flakes are lightly toasted, then remove them from oven to cool.

3. Add all the ingredients except for the coconut flakes to a 4-quart saucepan and heat over medium high heat until bubbles begin to form around the edges of the pan. You should be whisking while this is cooking to help the sugar dissolve, as well as to keep things from burning on the edges and bottom.

4. Remove the pan from the heat and let it cool for 30 minutes.

1 cup unsweetened coconut flakes (36g)

1 (13.5-ounce) can full-fat coconut milk (400ml)

1¾ cups full-fat coconut cream (420ml)

1 teaspoon pure vanilla extract (5ml)

½ cup coconut palm sugar (81g)

5. Pour the mixture into a refrigerator-safe container and cover. Chill for at least 6 hours; chilling overnight is best.

6. Churn the ice cream according to the manufacturer's instructions.

7. While the ice cream is churning, chop the coconut flakes into smaller pieces.

8. Add the chopped coconut to the churning ice cream during the last 2 to 3 minutes of churning time.

9. Scoop the ice cream into a freezer safe container and freeze for 2 to 3 hours to let the ice cream harden up before serving.

~ PUMPKIN PIE SPICE ~
ICE CREAM

MAKES 1 QUART

Have you noticed how pumpkin pie-flavored food starts rolling out in early September? Being an old-fashioned kind of girl, I think it should wait until closer to Thanksgiving. This Pumpkin Pie Spice Ice Cream also squashes the backlash of only using the pie seasonings because it DOES include actual pumpkin in the recipe. It's a great addition too, because it gives the ice cream a rich flavor. Now you can break out the pumpkin flavor any time of year.

1. Whisk all of the ice cream ingredients together in a 4-quart pot.

2. Cook the mixture over medium heat and bring to just a simmer (about 10 to 15 minutes). While this is cooking you will need to whisk it from time to time to keep the mixture from sticking to the sides and bottom of the pan.

3. Since you're making a custard, you want it to be between 160 to 170 degrees Fahrenheit (71 to 77 degrees Celsius). To see if your custard is done, simply dip a spoon into the mixture and run your finger down the back of the spoon. If the line stays clean, your custard is done. If the line blurs again, you need a little more time to make the custard.

1 ¼ cups full-fat coconut cream (300 ml)

1 cup full-fat coconut milk (240 ml)

⅓ cup pure maple syrup (80 ml)

⅓ cup organic canned pumpkin (80 ml)

4 large egg yolks

2 teaspoons ground cinnamon (2.6 g)

2 teaspoons ground ginger (1.7 g)

½ teaspoon pure vanilla extract

½ teaspoon ground allspice

½ teaspoon ground nutmeg

¼ teaspoon ground cloves

Pinch of sea salt

4. Remove the pot from the heat and let it cool for at least 30 minutes. Pour the mixture into a refrigerator-safe container and cover with plastic wrap, making sure the plastic wrap is covering the top of the liquid (this keeps a skin from forming on top of your custard). Place this into the refrigerator and chill for at least 6 hours. Chilling overnight is best.

5. If the custard separates while cooling, simply stir it before pouring it into the ice cream maker.

6. Pour the chilled mixture into an ice cream maker and process according to the manufacturer's instructions.

7. Transfer the ice cream to an airtight, freezer safe container and freeze for 2 to 3 hours before serving.

MOUNDS OF COCONUT
~ CHOCOLATE ~
ALMOND
ICE CREAM

MAKES 1 QUART

Remember when I said I was cuckoo for coconut? Well, I did it again with this one. This coconut ice cream is jam-packed with chocolate-covered almonds and more flakes of coconut. Yes, it's just like that famous candy bar, but in ice cream form.

1. Finely chop ½ cup toasted coconut flakes and set aside.

2. Bring coconut cream and coconut milk to a simmer in a heavy-bottomed pot. Remove the mixture from the heat and add 1 cup toasted coconut flakes. Stir, cover the pan, and let the coconut steep for 2 hours.

3. Whisk the egg yolks, maple syrup, vanilla, and salt together into a 4-quart heavy-bottomed pan. Strain the coconut mixture into the egg mixture (throw out the coconut). Cook over medium heat and bring to just a simmer (about 10 to 15 minutes). While this is cooking you will need to whisk it to keep the mixture from sticking to the sides and bottom of the pan.

1 ½ cups toasted coconut flakes (128g), divided

1 ¾ cups full-fat coconut cream (415ml)

1 (13.5-ounce) can full-fat coconut milk (400ml)

4 large egg yolks

½ cup maple syrup (120ml)

1 teaspoon pure vanilla extract (5ml)

Pinch of sea salt

4. Since you're making a custard, you want it to be between 160 to 170 degrees Fahrenheit (71 to 77 degrees Celsius). To see if your custard is done, simply dip a spoon into the mixture and run your finger down the back of the spoon. If the line stays clean, your custard is done. If the line blurs again, you need a little more time to make the custard.

5. Remove the pot from the heat and let it cool for at least 30 minutes. Pour the mixture into a refrigerator-safe container and cover with plastic wrap, making sure the plastic wrap is covering the top of the liquid (this keeps a skin from forming on top of your custard). Place this into the refrigerator and chill for at least 6 hours. Chilling overnight is best.

6. If the custard separates while cooling, simply stir it before pouring it into the ice cream maker.

FOR THE CHOCOLATE-COVERED ALMONDS

¼ cup unsweetened cocoa powder (21g)

5 tablespoons coconut oil (52g)

2 teaspoons maple syrup (13g)

¾ cup toasted whole almonds (106g)

7. Mix the cocoa powder, coconut oil, and maple syrup together. Make sure all the lumps are out of the mixture. Arrange the almonds in a single layer on a parchment paper-lined baking sheet. Pour the chocolate mixture over top of the roasted almonds. Use a spoon to move the almonds around and make sure that they all are covered with the chocolate, then spread them back out into a single layer. Place the baking sheet into the freezer while the ice cream is chilling.

8. Just before you begin to churn the ice cream, bring the chocolate-coated almonds out of the freezer and roughly chop them. Make sure that none of the pieces are too big. You don't want to bite into a big hunk of frozen nut. Then put them back into the freezer.

9. Begin churning the ice cream according to the manufacturer's instructions.

10. Add the chocolate covered almonds to the ice cream during the last 2 to 3 minutes of churning. Then add in the chopped coconut after the almonds and make sure everything is well mixed in.

11. Scoop the ice cream into a lidded container and freeze for 3 to 4 hours before serving.

~ BANANAS FOSTER ~
ICE CREAM

MAKES 1 QUART

I do love me some bananas foster. Maybe it's all the drama that surrounds it in a restaurant, as they bring the pan out with the flaming bananas. This recipe won't endanger your kitchen, but it will give you the flavor of that classic bananas foster dish. To take it right over the top, you can pour some of the caramel from the Nut 'n Honey recipe on it before serving. That will give it that "caramelly" glaze that you see on bananas foster when you flambé it.

1. Preheat the oven to 400 degrees Fahrenheit (204 degrees Celsius).

2. Toss the bananas and dates together in the coconut oil and arrange them in a single layer on a parchment paper–lined baking sheet. Bake for 20 to 25 minutes or until you see the bananas beginning to brown and soften.

3. Remove the fruit from oven and let it cool completely.

4. While the bananas are cooking, add the milk, cream, and egg yolks to a 4-quart saucepan and cook over medium heat until they just come to a simmer (about 10 to 15 minutes). While this is cooking you will need to whisk it to keep the mixture from sticking to the sides and bottom of the pan.

---

6 ripe medium bananas (peeled and sliced lengthwise)

½ cup whole dates, pitted (approximately 12 pitted dates) (140g)

2 tablespoons coconut oil (27g)

1 (13.5-ounce) can full-fat coconut milk (400ml)

1¾ cups full-fat coconut cream (420ml)

6 large egg yolks

1 teaspoon pure vanilla extract (5ml)

Pinch of sea salt

5. Since you're making a custard, you want it to be between 160 to 170 degrees Fahrenheit (71 to 77 degrees Celsius). To see if your custard is done, simply dip a spoon into the mixture and run your finger down the back of the spoon. If the line stays clean, your custard is done. If the line blurs again, you need a little more time to make the custard.

6. Pour the bananas, dates, and custard into a blender along with the vanilla and salt and buzz until everything is smooth; then stir this mixture into the custard mixture from the previous steps.

7. Pour the mixture into a refrigerator-safe container and cover with plastic wrap, making sure the plastic wrap is covering the top of the liquid (this keeps a skin from forming on top of your custard). Place this into the refrigerator and chill for at least 6 hours. Chilling overnight is best.

8. Pour the chilled mixture into an ice cream maker and process according to the manufacturer's instructions.

9. Transfer the ice cream to an airtight, freezer-safe container and freeze for 3 to 4 hours before serving.

10. Top with Nut 'n Honey caramel sauce if you like.

~ ROASTED BERRY ~
ICE CREAM

MAKES 1 QUART

I get it: *roasted berries* just sounds weird. Who roasts berries? Well, I do, and you will too, because you definitely want to make this ice cream. When you roast berries it super concentrates their flavor, turning what was once a light flavor into an incredibly strong one. The fun thing about this recipe is that you can change the flavor by mixing up the proportions of the different berries you use. Make it a little sweeter by using more strawberries, or make it a little more tart by using more raspberries and blackberries. The choice is yours.

1. Preheat the oven to 450 degrees Fahrenheit (240 degrees Celsius).

2. Roughly chop the strawberries. Place all of the berries on a parchment paper–lined baking sheet, and roast for 20 minutes.

3. Remove the berries from the oven and let them cool a bit.

4. Add the berries, maple syrup, milk, cream, vanilla, and salt to a blender and buzz until everything is smooth and creamy. If you don't like seeds in your ice cream, this is the time you will want to strain them out.

5. Pour the puréed berries into a bowl. Fill a larger bowl with ice and place the smaller bowl into the ice to chill. Let the berry purée chill like this for 45 minutes. It should feel slightly cold to the touch.

4 cups mixed berries (strawberries, raspberries, blackberries, and blueberries) (960g)

½ cup maple syrup (120ml)

1 cup cashew milk (240ml)

1 cup full-fat coconut cream (240ml)

1 teaspoon pure vanilla extract (5ml)

Pinch of sea salt

6. Give the mixture a good stir, then pour it into the ice cream maker and process according to the manufacturer's instructions.

7. Scoop the ice cream into an airtight container and freeze for 2 to 3 hours before serving.

~ BERRY SWIRL ~
ICE CREAM
MAKES 1 QUART

What could taste better than a sweet creamy ice cream swirled with fresh berries? This ice cream has the best of both worlds . . . sweet and tart. I love how—after you've eaten the velvetty ice cream—you get a jolt of tart from the berries. Not too much—just a little bit to make you sit up and take notice.

1 (13.5-ounce) can full-fat coconut milk (400ml)

1 ¾ cups full-fat coconut cream (420ml)

⅓ cup maple syrup (104g)

1 teaspoon pure vanilla extract (5ml)

Pinch of sea salt

½ cup raspberries fresh or frozen, thawed (60g)

½ cup blueberries fresh or frozen, thawed (85g)

1 tablespoon coconut palm sugar (10g)

1. Add the coconut milk, cream, maple syrup, vanilla, and salt to a 4-quart saucepan and heat over medium-high heat until bubbles begin to form around the edges of pan. Whisk the mixture while it's cooking to keep it from burning on the edges and bottom of the pan.

2. Remove the mixture from heat and let it cool for 30 minutes.

3. Pour the mixture into a refrigerator-safe container and cover. Chill for at least 6 hours. Chilling overnight is best.

4. Place the raspberries and blueberries into a small bowl along with the coconut sugar. Mash the berries and mix the sugar into their juices. Place the bowl in the refrigerator along with the ice cream base.

5. Churn the ice cream according to the manufacturer's instructions.

6. Scoop half of the ice cream into a freezer safe container and pour the berries over the top, then top the berries with the remaining ice cream and freeze for 3–4 hours to let the ice cream harden up before serving.

~ KEY LIME PIE ~
ICE CREAM

MAKES 1 QUART

With the palm trees swaying and the trade winds blowing, what could be a more appropriate dish than a big ol' piece of key lime pie? How about a frozen version . . . it'll cool you off faster too! This key lime pie has the tang of lime and bit of a coconut flavor to keep that tropical vibe flowing. I can hear the ocean waves now, can't you?

1. Whisk all of the ice cream ingredients together in a 4-quart pot.

2. Cook over medium heat and bring to just a simmer (about 10 to 15 minutes). While this is cooking you will need to whisk it from time to time to keep the mixture from sticking to the sides and bottom of the pan.

3. Since you're making a custard, you want it to be between 160 to 170 degrees Fahrenheit (71 to 77 degrees Celsius). To see if your custard is done, simply dip a spoon into the mixture and run your finger down the back of the spoon. If the line stays clean, your custard is done. If the line blurs again, you need a little more time to make the custard.

1 tablespoon coconut oil (15ml)

1 (13.5-ounce) can full-fat coconut milk (400ml)

¼ cup raw honey (60ml)

1 tablespoon lime zest (from approximately 2 limes) (15g)

½ cup freshly squeezed lime juice (from 3–4 limes) (120ml)

6 large egg yolks

Pinch of sea salt

4. Remove from heat and let cool, at least 30 minutes. Pour into a refrigerator-safe container and cover with plastic wrap, making sure the plastic wrap is covering the top of the liquid (this keeps a skin from forming on top of your custard). Place this into the refrigerator and chill for at least 6 hours. Overnight is best.

5. If the custard separates while cooling, simply stir it before pouring it into the ice cream maker.

6. Pour the chilled mixture into the ice cream maker and process according to the manufacturer's instructions.

7. Transfer the ice cream to an airtight, freezer-safe container and freeze for 2 to 3 hours before serving.

NO-CHURN
STRAWBERRY
ICE CREAM

MAKES 1 QUART

Who needs an ice cream maker? Not you when you make this fresh strawberry ice cream. The key to making this super-delicious treat is to use strawberries when they're in season, as they really are the star of this show. The berries are surrounded by a light, airy, creamy coconut that only brings out more of the strawberry flavor.

1. Chill the mixing bowl, beater/whisk, and coconut cream really well before starting this recipe. The colder these things are, the better your ice cream will turn out.

2. Pour 2 cups (480 ml) coconut cream into the mixing bowl and beat just until stiff peaks form.

3. Add the honey, vanilla, and the rest of the cream to the bowl and beat until stiff peaks form again.

4. Carefully fold the strawberries into the whipped cream mixture.

5. Spread the mixture into a freezer safe container and freeze for 2 to 3 hours for a frozen mousse-like treat or overnight for a firmer ice cream.

2½ cups full-fat coconut cream (chilled) (600ml), divided

½ cup raw honey (120ml)

1 teaspoon pure vanilla extract (5ml)

1 pound strawberries (cut berries into 8 pieces and lightly smash about ⅔ of the berries) (455g)

~ BLUEBERRY CRISP ~
ICE CREAM

MAKES 1 QUART

A blueberry crisp, topped with vanilla ice cream, is one of my all-time favorite desserts. So I thought, why not put everything I love about the dessert into an ice cream? Voilà, Blueberry Crisp Ice Cream was born. The crisp part comes from a layer of Paleo granola that stays crunchy even in the frozen ice cream. Now you can get all the flavors from a baked dessert straight out of your freezer.

1. Preheat oven to 300 degrees Fahrenheit (148 degrees Celsius).

2. Add the walnuts, cashews, pumpkin seeds, and coconut to a blender and pulse just enough to break everything up into small pieces. You don't want to turn this into a paste—it should be chunky.

3. In a large mixing bowl, whisk the egg white and water until they are nice and frothy. Now whisk in the honey, oil, vanilla, and salt.

4. Pour the nut mixture into the bowl and mix until everything is well coated with the honey mixture.

5. Spread the mixture onto a parchment paper-lined baking sheet. Try to keep the thickness even (the thinner the better—it will cook faster).

FOR THE GRANOLA

1 cup raw walnuts (128g)

1 cup raw cashews (113g)

1 cup raw pumpkin seeds (118g)

½ cup raw unsweetened coconut flakes (18g)

1 large egg white

1 tablespoon water (15ml)

⅓ cup raw honey (106ml)

3 tablespoons walnut oil (45ml)

½ teaspoon pure vanilla extract

¼ teaspoon sea salt

6. Bake for 20 to 30 minutes or until golden brown and getting crispy. You'll need to stir the mixture around about every 10 minutes to keep things cooking evenly.

7. Remove the mixture from the oven and let it cool for 10 to 15 minutes.

8. Use a spatula to release the granola and store it in an airtight container. (You'll have way more granola than you'll need for this ice cream recipe.)

1¼ cups cashew milk (300ml)

1 (13.5-ounce) can full-fat coconut milk (400ml)

⅓ cup coconut palm sugar (53g)

⅛ teaspoon grated nutmeg

¼ teaspoon sea salt

9. Pour the milks, sugar, nutmeg, and salt into a 4-quart pan and heat over medium-high heat. Bring to a simmer.

10. Whisk while the mixture is cooking and continue to cook until the sugar is dissolved, then remove from the heat.

11. Let the mixture cool for 30 minutes and then pour it into a refrigerator-safe container with a lid. Cover the container and chill in the refrigerator for at least 6 hours. Chilling overnight is best.

FOR THE BLUEBERRY SWIRL

1 cup blueberries (fresh or frozen, thawed) (170g)

¼ cup coconut palm sugar (40g)

¼–½ cup granola (from earlier in recipe) (50–100g)

12. Drop the blueberries and sugar into a bowl and mash them together.

13. Pop the mixture into the refrigerator to chill.

14. Pour the ice cream base mixture into the ice cream maker and churn according to the manufacturer's instructions.

15. Spoon and spread ⅓ of the ice cream into your freezer container.

16. Spoon and spread some of the blueberry mixture on top of the ice cream. Then sprinkle with some of the granola.

17. Repeat steps 15 and 16.

18. Finish by spreading a layer of ice cream on top.

19. Place the ice cream into the freezer for at least 4 hours before serving.

~ MATCHA ~
ICE CREAM

MAKES 1 PINT

If you're a fan of matcha/green tea, then this ice cream is calling—no, screaming—your name. There is no mistaking the flavor once you take a bite, and its gorgeous green color is like a siren song to your taste buds. I like to drizzle my bowl of matcha ice cream with a little chocolate, but that's just me. You can eat it as is or drizzle it with your favorite flavor.

1. In a 4-quart saucepan, mix all of the ingredients except the matcha together and heat them over medium high heat.

2. Whisk in the matcha (green tea powder).

3. Continue cooking until the mixture is hot but not boiling, then remove from the heat.

4. Pour the mixture into a lidded container to cool, then cover and refrigerate overnight.

5. Pour the mixture into the ice cream maker and process according to the ice cream manufacturer's instructions.

6. Scoop the ice cream into a freezer-safe container and freeze for 3 to 4 hours before serving.

1 (13.5-ounce) can full-fat coconut milk (400ml)

½ cup maple syrup (120ml)

½ teaspoon freshly squeezed lemon juice

Pinch of sea salt

2 tablespoons matcha (green tea powder) (30g)

~ BASIL ~
ICE CREAM
WITH ROASTED STRAWBERRIES AND BALSAMIC REDUCTION

MAKES 1 PINT

Basil ice cream sounds a bit strange, I'll admit, but I've been eating it for quite some time now. Basil has a sweet, earthy flavor that works really well with the cream and milk in this recipe. You can eat this ice cream on its own and you'll completely stump your friends when you ask them to tell you what they taste. But I really love serving this with roasted strawberries on top and a swirl of balsamic vinegar reduction (the balsamic sweetens when it's reduced). This is also good with chocolate syrup.

24 large basil leaves (washed and dried)

1 cup cashew cream (240ml)

1 (13.5-ounce) can full-fat coconut milk (400ml)

4 egg yolks

½ cup raw honey (120ml)

Pinch of sea salt

12 strawberries

½ cup balsamic vinegar (120ml)

1. Remove the basil leaves from the stems and cut them into a chiffonade (to chiffonade the basil, simply stack 4 to 5 leaves on top of one another and roll them up lengthwise. Then take your knife and cut the rolled leaves into thin strips).

2. Bring the cashew cream and coconut milk to a simmer in a heavy-bottomed pot. Remove the mixture from the heat and add the chopped basil. Stir, cover the pan, and let the basil steep for 2 hours.

3. Whisk the egg yolks, honey, and salt together in a heavy-bottomed pan. Strain the basil mixture into the egg mixture (throw out the basil). Cook over

medium heat and bring to just a simmer (about 10 to 15 minutes). While this is cooking you will need to whisk it to keep the mixture from sticking to the sides and bottom of the pan.

4. Since you're making a custard, you want it to be between 160 to 170 degrees Fahrenheit (71 to 77 degrees Celsius). To see if your custard is done, simply dip a spoon into the mixture and run your finger down the back of the spoon. If the line stays clean, your custard is done. If the line blurs again, you need a little more time to make the custard.

5. Remove from heat and let cool, at least 30 minutes. Pour into a refrigerator-safe container and cover with plastic wrap, making sure the plastic wrap is covering the top of the liquid (this keeps a skin from forming on top of your custard). Place this into the refrigerator and chill for at least 6 hours. Overnight is best.

6. Pour the ice cream base mixture into the ice cream maker and churn according to the manufacturer's instructions.

7. Scoop the ice cream into a lidded container and freeze for 3 to 4 hours before serving.

8. While the ice cream is freezing, preheat your oven to 400 degrees Fahrenheit (204 degrees Celsius).

9. Wash, hull, and slice the strawberries in half, then arrange them in a single layer on a parchment paper–lined baking sheet.

10. Bake the strawberries for 20 to 25 minutes or until you see that they are no longer shiny and have shrunk a bit.

11. Remove the strawberries from the oven and let them cool.

12. Pour the balsamic vinegar into a small, heavy-bottomed pan and heat over medium heat. Cook the vinegar until it has reduced by half. Keep an eye on it, because once it starts reducing the process goes very quickly, and you could end up with just a burnt layer of vinegar on your pan.

13. Remove the vinegar from the heat and let it cool.

14. Serve the basil ice cream topped with slices of the roasted strawberries and a drizzle of balsamic vinegar reduction.

~ MINT CHIP ~
ICE CREAM

MAKES 1 PINT

This isn't the same ol', same ol' mint chip ice cream. This stuff is made with real deal mint. It's got that great mint flavor, but you'll notice a fresh taste at the end. That tells you it was made with real mint and not some kind of weird extract. Oh, and the little* chocolate bits in there are the icing on the cake (er . . . ice cream). So dish yourself out a big bowl of this ice cream and enjoy.

FOR THE ICE CREAM

1 cup cashew cream (240ml)

1 (13.5-ounce) can full-fat coconut milk (400ml)

⅔ ounce fresh mint (thoroughly washed and dried)** (18.7g)

4 egg yolks

½ cup raw honey (120ml)

Pinch of sea salt

FOR THE CHOCOLATE

½ cup unsweetened cocoa powder (21g)

5 tablespoons coconut oil (52g)

2 teaspoons maple syrup (13g)

1. Chop the mint leaves into small pieces and discard the stems.

2. Bring the cashew cream and coconut milk to a simmer in a heavy-bottomed pot. Remove the mixture from the heat and add the chopped mint. Stir, cover the pan, and let the mint steep for 2 hours.

3. Whisk the egg yolks, honey, and salt together in a heavy-bottomed pan. Strain the mint mixture into the egg mixture (throw out the mint).

4. Since you're making a custard, you want it to be between 160 to 170 degrees Fahrenheit (71 to 77 degrees Celsius). To see if your custard is done,

---

* For bigger chunks of chocolate in the ice cream you can mix up the cocoa powder, coconut oil, and maple syrup and spread it onto a parchment paper-lined baking sheet. Put the sheet into the freezer for a few minutes, then take it out and break the chocolate into pieces. Add the chocolate pieces to the ice cream during the last 1 to 2 minutes of churning.

** If the package is mostly mint leaves, use half of the package. If the package is mostly thick stems, then use all of the leaves.

simply dip a spoon into the mixture and run your finger down the back of the spoon. If the line stays clean, your custard is done. If the line blurs again, you need a little more time to make the custard.

5. Remove from heat and let cool, at least 30 minutes. Pour into a refrigerator-safe container and cover with plastic wrap, making sure the plastic wrap is covering the top of the liquid (this keeps a skin from forming on top of your custard). Place this into the refrigerator and chill for at least 6 hours. Overnight is best.

6. If the custard separates while cooling, simply stir it before pouring it into the ice cream maker.

7. Begin churning the ice cream in your ice cream maker according to the manufacturer's instructions. While the ice cream is churning, mix the cocoa powder, coconut oil, and maple syrup together in a small bowl.

8. Slowly drizzle the chocolate into the churning ice cream during the last 2 to 3 minutes of the churning time. (You may not need to use all of the chocolate.)

9. Scoop the ice cream into a lidded container and freeze for 3 to 4 hours before serving.

EXTREME CHOCOLATE
ICE CREAM

MAKES 1 QUART

I know there are some chocoholics out there. Who are you? Raise your hands. This ice cream uses two kinds of chocolate to bring out all the rich chocolate flavor. It's got a subtle sweetness that won't leave you thinking you've just eaten a container of kiddie ice cream. No, this is very adult . . . but the kids will find it just sweet enough that they'll like it too. If you want to share, that is.

1. Chop the chocolate into small pieces and add them to a small bowl along with the maple syrup. Melt the chocolate in the microwave for 30-second intervals. Give the chocolate a good stir between each interval. Set aside once it's melted.

2. In a 4-quart pot, beat the egg yolks and then add the cream, milk, coconut sugar, cocoa powder, and melted chocolate. Whisk to combine.

3. Cook the mixture over medium heat and bring it to just a simmer (about 10 to 15 minutes). While this is cooking you will need to whisk it to keep the mixture from sticking to the sides and bottom of the pan.

2 ounces unsweetened baker's chocolate (56g)

2 tablespoons maple syrup (30ml)

4 large egg yolks

2 cups coconut cream (480ml)

1 cup full-fat coconut milk (240ml)

½ cup coconut palm sugar (81g)

⅓ cup unsweetened cocoa powder (27g)

1 teaspoon pure vanilla extract (5ml)

Pinch of sea salt

4. Since you're making a custard, you want it to be between 160 to 170 degrees Fahrenheit (71 to 77 degrees Celsius). To see if your custard is done, simply dip a spoon into the mixture and run your finger down the back of the spoon. If the line stays clean, your custard is done. If the line blurs again, you need a little more time to make the custard.

5. Remove from heat and let cool, at least 30 minutes. Pour into a refrigerator-safe container and cover with plastic wrap, making sure the plastic wrap is covering the top of the liquid (this keeps a skin from forming on top of your custard). Place this into the refrigerator and chill for at least 6 hours. Overnight is best.

6. Pour the ice cream base mixture into the ice cream maker and churn according to the manufacturer's instructions.

7. Scoop the ice cream into a lidded container and freeze for 3 to 4 hours before serving.

~ COCOA RICHE ~
ICE CREAM

MAKES 1 PINT

Cocoa has its own flavor, distinct from chocolate, and this ice cream showcases that deep, rich flavor. It's a little icier than regular ice cream, which gives it more of an edginess. But don't we all strive to be a little bit edgier? I think this ice cream might be the start of something for you.

1. Add all the ingredients to a blender and buzz until well blended and very smooth.

2. Pour the mixture into a refrigerator-safe, lidded container, and place into the refrigerator to chill overnight.

3. Process the ice cream according to the ice cream maker manufacturer's instructions.

4. Scoop the ice cream into a freezer safe container, cover, and freeze for 2 to 3 hours before serving.

1 cup full-fat coconut milk (240ml)

1 cup cashew milk (240ml)

½ cup maple syrup (120ml)

¼ cup organic cocoa butter (freeze and grate the cocoa butter for easier measuring) (60g)

2 tablespoons coconut oil (30ml)

¼ cup unsweetened cocoa powder* (21g)

1 teaspoon pure vanilla extract (5ml)

Pinch of sea salt

1 tablespoon tapioca powder (7g)

* Make sure to use the best-quality cocoa powder you can in this recipe. It makes a big difference in the flavor of the ice cream.

CHOCOLATE ORANGE ICE CREAM

MAKES 1 PINT

If you're one who likes the combination of dark chocolate and orange, you're going to be really happy with this recipe. The deep rich chocolate flavor is accented by a hint of citrusy orange. It's not overly sweet and its flavors will have you wishing chocolate oranges really did grow on trees.

1. Chop the baker's chocolate finely and put it into a small bowl, and then add the 2 tablespoons maple syrup. Melt the chocolate by putting it into the microwave for 30-second intervals on the high setting. After each 30-second interval, stir the chocolate to help it melt. Continue doing this until the chocolate has melted, then set it aside.

2. Pour ¼ cup cashew milk into a small bowl and add the tapioca flour. Whisk the mixture to thoroughly combine the two ingredients and set aside.

3. In a 4-quart saucepan, add the coconut cream, remaining cashew milk, cocoa powder, melted chocolate, vanilla, orange zest, orange juice, and ¼ cup maple syrup. Whisk to thoroughly combine all of the ingredients.

2 ounces unsweetened baker's chocolate (57g)

¼ cup + 2 tablespoons maple syrup (39g), divided

1 cup cashew milk (240ml), divided

1 tablespoon tapioca flour (7g)

1 cup coconut cream (240ml)

½ cup unsweetened cocoa powder (42g)

1 tablespoon pure vanilla extract (15ml)

2½ teaspoons orange zest (13g)

½ cup orange juice (120ml)

Pinch of sea salt

4. Heat the mixture over medium heat and cook until small bubbles begin to appear around the edges of the pan.

5. Remove the mixture from the heat and whisk in the tapioca flour mixture and then the salt. You'll begin to see the mixture thicken up.

6. Let the mixture cool a bit, then cover the top of the mixture with plastic wrap. Chill in the refrigerator for at least 4 hours (overnight is best).

7. Pour the mixture into the ice cream maker and process according to the manufacturer's instructions.

8. Scoop the ice cream into a lidded container and freeze for 2 to 3 hours before serving.

NO-CHURN
~ MEXICAN ~
CHOCOLATE
ICE CREAM

MAKES 1 PINT

Sometimes you don't feel like lugging out all the heavy equipment from wherever you have it stored. This ice cream is light and airy but packed with chocolate flavor, and it doesn't require an ice cream maker. You'll really taste the cinnamon and allspice in here—they truly give it that spicy edge so true to Mexican chocolate. I didn't add a kick of heat to this recipe, but if you want to, you could add a dash of cayenne in there to ramp things up.

1. Chill mixing bowl, beater/whisk, and coconut cream well before starting this recipe. The colder these things are, the better your ice cream will turn out.

2. In a small bowl, mix together the honey, cocoa powder, melted chocolate, vanilla, cinnamon, allspice, and salt. Make sure you have all of the lumps worked out of the mixture, and then set it aside

3. Pour 2 cups (480 ml) coconut cream into the mixing bowl and beat just until stiff peaks form.

2½ cups full-fat coconut cream (600 ml), divided

⅓ cup pure raw honey (113 g)

¼ cup unsweetened cocoa powder (21 g)

2 ounces unsweetened baker's chocolate (melted) (56 g)

1 teaspoon pure vanilla extract (5 ml)

2 teaspoons ground cinnamon (5 g)

¼ teaspoon allspice

Pinch of sea salt

4. Add the chocolate mixture and the rest of the cream to the bowl and beat until stiff peaks form again.

5. Spread the mixture into a freezer-safe container and freeze for 2 to 3 hours for a frozen mousse-like treat, or overnight for a firmer ice cream.

~ BANANA CREAM ~
PIE

For the banana lovers we have this rich Banana Cream Pie. While the filling is loaded with banana goodness, the whipped cream keeps things nice and light. You shouldn't have to feel heavy after eating dessert. The crust has a nicely sweet crunch that pairs really well with the creamy banana filling.

FOR THE CRUST

1 cup packed pitted Deglet dates (approximately 24 pitted dates) (280g)

1 cup raw almonds (164g)

1 cup raw pecans (53g)

2 tablespoons maple syrup (30ml)

¼ teaspoon sea salt

FOR THE PIE FILLING

1 (13.5-ounce) can + ½ cup full-fat coconut cream (532ml)

3 ripe bananas (with brown spots on them)

2 tablespoons raw honey (30ml)

2 teaspoons pure vanilla extract (10ml)

1. Chill the coconut cream, whisk, and metal bowl in the refrigerator overnight. (This step helps ensure that you get a nice and fluffy whipped cream for the pie. If you can't fit the bowl in the refrigerator, at least chill the cream and the beater[s].)

2. Roughly chop the pitted dates and toss them into the bowl of a food processor.

3. Add the remaining crust ingredients to the food processor, then process the ingredients until they come together into a large clump or a couple of clumps.

4. Remove the crust ingredients from the food processor and gently press them into a 9-inch tart pan with a removable bottom (you can make the pie in a regular 9-inch pie pan, but it's easier to cut and remove pieces from the tart pan since the bottom lifts the pie out away from the edges of the pan). Press the ingredients into the pan and up the sides evenly, and then set the pan aside.

5. Clean the food processor, because you'll need it to make the pie filling.

6. Peel the bananas and break them into pieces before dropping them into the bowl of the food processor. Add the honey to the bananas, then process until the bananas are puréed and set them aside.

7. Pull the cream, beaters, and bowl from the refrigerator and add the cream and vanilla extract to the chilled bowl. Whip until stiff peaks form in the cream (a stiff peak is reached when you lift the whisk/beaters from the cream and a peak forms that stands up straight and doesn't fall over).

8. Remove ½ to ¾ cup of the whipped cream and set it aside.

9. Slowly pour the puréed bananas down the side of the mixing bowl and into the cream. Carefully fold the bananas into the whipped cream.

10. Once the bananas are completely folded into the cream, pour the mixture into the prepared pie crust. Use your spatula to smooth out the top.

11. Spoon the set-aside whipped cream into the middle of the pie and use a spoon to form little peaks in the cream.

12. Place the pie onto a baking sheet and place it in the freezer (make sure the pie is level). Freeze the pie overnight before serving.

13. Let the pie rest at room temperature for 15 to 20 minutes before cutting and serving it.*

---

* For an even prettier presentation, thinly slice a banana and arrange slices around a ring of whipped cream on the pie.

～ CHOCOLATE CREAM ～
PIE

MAKES 8 SERVINGS

This rich and creamy chocolate pie screams chocolate! With two kinds of chocolate in the pie and then a crunchy, crumbly chocolate crust, this pie takes chocolate right to the top. You'll love the contrast between the creamy filling and the crunchy crust.

1. Chill the coconut cream, whisk, and metal bowl in the refrigerator overnight. (This step helps to ensure that you get a nice and fluffy whipped cream for the pie. If you can't fit the bowl in the refrigerator, at least chill the cream and the whisk/beater(s).)

2. Roughly chop the pitted dates and toss them into the bowl of a food processor.

3. Add the remaining crust ingredients to the food processor, then process the ingredients until they come together. The mixture should stick together when you press it between your fingers. Add another tablespoon of water and pulse if the mixture isn't coming together.

FOR THE CRUST

1 cup packed pitted Deglet dates (approximately 24 pitted dates) (280g)

1½ cups raw almonds (216g)

⅓ cup unsweetened cocoa powder (28g)

¼ teaspoon sea salt

2 tablespoons water (10ml)

FOR THE PIE FILLING

1 (13.5-ounce) can full-fat coconut cream (414ml)

2 ounces unsweetened baker's chocolate (57g)

⅓ cup unsweetened cocoa powder (28g)

⅓ cup pure maple syrup (80ml)

1 teaspoon pure vanilla extract (5ml)

4. Tear two 3-inch wide strips of parchment paper into long strips and lay them into a 9-inch pie pan, forming an X. Now tear two pieces of plastic wrap and press into the pie pan on top of the parchment paper X. This will make it easy to lift the frozen pie out of the pan for cutting.

5. Remove the crust ingredients from the food processor and gently press them into the prepared 9-inch pie pan. Press the ingredients into the pan and up the sides evenly, then set the pan aside.

6. Chop the baker's chocolate into small pieces and place them into a microwave-safe bowl. Heat on high setting for 30-second intervals. In between each heating, stir the chocolate to help it melt. Repeat these steps until the chocolate is melted (should only take two or three intervals).

7. Stir the cocoa powder and maple syrup into the melted chocolate and whisk until all of the lumps are gone, then set it aside.

8. Pull the cream, beaters, and bowl from the refrigerator and add the cream and vanilla extract to the chilled bowl. Whip until stiff peaks form in the cream (a stiff peak is reached when you lift the whisk/beaters from the cream and a peak forms that stands up straight and doesn't fall over).

9. Scoop out ½ cup whipped cream and set it aside.

10. Slowly add the chocolate mixture down the side of the mixing bowl with the whipped cream. Beat just until the chocolate is thoroughly mixed into the cream.

11. Spoon the chocolate whipped cream into the pie crust and use a spoon or spatula to smooth the top.

12. Now spoon the ½ cup plain whipped cream onto the top of the pie and drag a knife through it to make swirls on top of the pie.

13. Put the pie onto a baking sheet and place in the freezer (make sure the pie is level). Freeze overnight before serving.

14. Let the pie rest for 15 to 20 minutes at room temperature before cutting and serving it.

15. Serve with more whipped coconut cream, chocolate shavings, and toasted coconut.

HEATHER'S
~ MOCHA
ALMOND FUDGE
PIE

MAKES 8 SERVINGS

My friend Heather loves any and everything mocha, so I made this pie with her in mind. Of course, it's got chocolate in the fudge topping, filling, and crust, but the real star of this pie is the coffee. You'll find it in both the filling and crust, so you'll get that rich mocha flavor in every bite.

FOR THE FUDGE SAUCE

½ cup maple syrup (240ml)

2 tablespoons water (30ml)

6¾ ounces full-fat coconut milk (200ml)

1 teaspoon pure vanilla extract (5ml)

⅓ cup unsweetened cocoa powder (61g)

1. Chill the coconut cream, whisk, and metal bowl in the refrigerator overnight. (This step helps to ensure that you get a nice and fluffy whipped cream for the pie. If you can't fit the bowl in the refrigerator, at least chill the cream and the whisk/beater(s).)

2. To make the fudge sauce, add maple syrup and water to 4- or 5-quart pot and bring to a boil over medium-high heat. Cover the pot for 2 minutes (this keeps sugar crystals from forming on the sides of the pot).

3. Remove the cover and keep cooking and swirling the pot until you get a deep amber color, approximately 90 seconds (the bubbles will change color too).

4. Add the coconut milk and vanilla to the mixture, then whisk and remove the pan from the heat (the mixture may bubble quite violently when you add the coconut milk; keep whisking until it settles down). Add the cocoa powder and whisk until thoroughly combined and smooth. Set the pot aside to cool to room temperature.

5. Roughly chop the pitted dates and toss them into the bowl of a food processor.

6. Add the remaining ingredients to the food processor and then process the ingredients until they come together. The mixture should stick together when you press it between your fingers. Add another tablespoon of coffee and pulse only if the mixture isn't coming together.

7. Remove the crust ingredients from the food processor and gently press them into an 8-inch springform pan. Press the ingredients into the pan and up the sides evenly, and then set it aside.

8. Chop the baker's chocolate into small pieces and place them into a microwave-safe bowl. Heat on high setting for 30-second intervals. In between each heating, stir the chocolate to help it melt. Repeat these steps until chocolate is melted (should only take 2 or 3 intervals), then set it aside.

FOR THE CRUST

1 cup packed pitted Deglet dates (approximately 24 pitted dates) (280g)

1½ cups raw almonds (246g)

⅓ cup unsweetened cocoa powder (28g)

¼ teaspoon sea salt

2 tablespoons coffee (30ml), plus more if needed

FOR THE FILLING

1 (13.5-ounce) can full-fat coconut cream (chilled) (414ml)

3 ounces unsweetened baker's chocolate (86g)

⅓ cup pure maple syrup 80ml)

1 tablespoon + 2 teaspoons instant espresso powder (10g)

1 teaspoon pure vanilla extract (5ml)

9. Pull the cream, beaters, and bowl from the refrigerator and add the cream, maple syrup, espresso powder, and vanilla extract to the chilled bowl. Whip until stiff peaks form in the cream (a stiff peak is reached when you lift the whisk/beaters from the cream and a peak forms that stands up straight and doesn't fall over).

10. Slowly add the chocolate mixture down the side of the bowl of the whipped cream mixture. Fold the chocolate into the cream mixture until the chocolate is thoroughly mixed into the cream.

11. Spoon the mocha whipped cream into the crust and use a spoon or spatula to smooth the top.

12. Now spoon the fudge sauce on top of the pie. You can use as little or as much as you like. You'll probably have some of the fudge sauce left over.

13. Sprinkle with toasted sliced almonds.

14. Place the pie onto a baking sheet place in the freezer (make sure the pie is level). Freeze overnight before serving.

15. Let the pie rest for 15 to 20 minutes at room temperature before cutting and serving it.

FOR THE TOPPING

½ cup toasted sliced almonds (70g)

~ BAKED ALASKA ~

MAKES 8 SERVINGS

Baked Alaska isn't just Neapolitan ice cream on a cake slathered in meringue. We're taking this Baked Alaska to new heights by filling it with fresh blackberry ice cream and a blackberry sauce. And just in case you thought you couldn't make magical meringue Paleo friendly . . . you can. It's not covered with the snowy white meringue you're used to (due to the color of the coconut palm sugar), but it tastes just as delightful.

1. Preheat the oven to 350 degrees Fahrenheit (177 degrees Celsius).

2. Lightly coat an 8-inch cake pan with ghee. This will help prevent the cake from sticking.

3. Add the almond flour, starch, baking powder, baking soda, and salt to a bowl and whisk for 2 minutes. This will thoroughly mix all of the dry ingredients together and help prevent pockets from forming in the cake when you bake it.

4. In another bowl, thoroughly whisk the maple syrup, coconut milk, eggs, and vanilla together.

5. Pour the wet ingredients into the dry ingredients and stir to thoroughly combine.

6. Now pour the cake ingredients into the prepared cake pan and slide the pan into the oven. Bake for 30 to 35 minutes or until a toothpick inserted into the middle of the cake comes out clean.

FOR THE CAKE*

Ghee, for greasing

1 ½ cups almond flour (129g)

¼ cup + 2 tablespoons tapioca starch (42g)

1 teaspoon baking powder (5g)

1 teaspoon baking soda (5g)

½ teaspoon sea salt

3 tablespoons maple syrup (45ml)

1 cup full-fat coconut milk (237ml)

4 large eggs

2 teaspoons pure vanilla extract (10ml)

* Inspired by http://www.agrainofsalt.net/basic-paleo-sponge-cake

FOR THE BLACKBERRY SAUCE

6 ounces fresh blackberries
  (170g)

2 tablespoons raw honey (30ml)

1 teaspoon freshly squeezed
  lemon juice (5ml)

FOR THE ICE CREAM

12 ounces fresh blackberries
  (340g)

¼ cup raw honey (60ml)

1 tablespoon freshly squeezed
  lemon juice (15ml)

1 cup cashew cream (240ml)

1 (13.5-ounce) can full-fat
  coconut milk (414ml)

4 large egg yolks

½ teaspoon sea salt

7. Set the cake aside to cool for 10 minutes. Run a knife around the edge of the cake to help loosen it from the pan, and turn the cake out onto a rack to cool to room temperature.

8. Once the cake has cooled, trim cake to 1-inch thickness.

9. In a small pan add the blackberries, honey, and lemon juice. Heat over medium heat. While the mixture is heating, stir the mixture and mash the berries with the back of a fork. Continue cooking until the berries have broken down (are soft) and are completely mashed. Remove the pan from heat and strain the liquid into a bowl. Discard the skins and seeds and set the mixture aside to cool to room temperature.

10. In a small pan add the blackberries, honey, and lemon juice. Heat over medium heat. While the mixture is heating, stir the mixture and mash the berries with the back of a fork. Continue cooking until berries are soft, have broken down, and are completely mashed. Remove from heat and strain liquid into a bowl. Discard skins and seeds.

11. In a 4- or 5-quart pan add the blackberry juice, cream, milk, egg yolks, and salt.

12. Cook the mixture over medium heat and bring to just a simmer (about 10 to 15 minutes). While this is cooking you will need to whisk it from time to time to keep the mixture from sticking to the sides and bottom of the pan.

13. Since you're making a custard, you want it to be between 160 to 170 degrees Fahrenheit (71 to 77 degrees Celsius). To see if your custard is done, simply dip a spoon into the mixture and run your finger down the back of the spoon. If the line stays clean, your custard is done. If the line blurs again, you need a little more time to make the custard.

14. Remove from heat and let cool, at least 30 minutes. Pour into a refrigerator-safe container and cover with plastic wrap, making sure the plastic wrap is covering the top of the liquid (this keeps a skin from forming on top of your custard). Place this into the refrigerator and chill for at least 6 hours. Overnight is best.

15. If the custard separates while cooling, simply stir it before pouring it into the ice cream maker.

16. Pour the chilled mixture into the ice cream maker and process according to the manufacturer's instructions.

17. Line a bowl (that's large enough to accommodate the cake . . . i.e. an 8-inch bowl) with plastic wrap. You may need to use 2 sheets to make sure the bowl is completely covered with the plastic wrap.

18. Spoon the ice cream into the bowl and use a spatula to push the ice cream into the bowl. Smooth the top layer.

19. Spoon about half of the blackberry sauce onto the cut top of cake. Keep the sauce inside the edges of the cake—don't let it drip down the sides. Use the rest of the sauce to top pancakes or waffles.

20. Carefully place the cake, sauce-side toward the ice cream, onto the ice cream. Gently press the cake into the ice cream so that they are firmly attached. Cover the whole thing tightly in plastic wrap.

21. Place the bowl into the freezer and freeze overnight.

FOR THE MERINGUE

½ cup coconut palm sugar (81 g)

¼ teaspoon cream of tartar

4 egg whites

22. Add the coconut palm sugar to the bowl of a food processor and buzz until the sugar is superfine.

23. Preheat the oven to 450 degrees Fahrenheit (232 degrees Celsius).

24. Add the cream of tartar and egg whites to a large bowl and beat using the medium speed of a mixer until soft peaks form (about 1 minute). Add sugar and beat until stiff peaks form again.

25. Take the cake out of the refrigerator, remove the plastic wrap, and turn out frozen cake onto the parchment paper (cake-side down). Remove the remaining plastic wrap from the cake. Completely cover the ice cream and cake with the meringue. Use a spatula to make swirls or peaks in the meringue. Bake until the meringue begins to brown, about 5 minutes. (Watch the browning process, because it may take less time in your oven. You just want the peaks of the meringue browned.) Using 2 spatulas, carefully transfer to a cake plate and serve immediately.

26. Alternatively, you could use a propane torch to brown the meringue. Follow the manufacturer's instructions to use the torch.

27. Please note that the egg whites in this recipe will not be fully cooked. If that is a concern for you, you can purchase pasteurized eggs to use in the meringue recipe.

~ AFFOGATO ~

MAKES 1 QUART

This isn't so much a recipe as it is another way to eat this delicious ice cream. Affogato is an Italian dessert of vanilla ice cream topped with a shot of espresso. If you don't have an espresso maker, you could top the ice cream with strong coffee. These two simple ingredients make for a delicious dessert.

FOR THE PURE VANILLA ICE CREAM

1 (13.5-ounce) can full-fat coconut milk (400ml)

1¾ cups full-fat coconut cream (420ml)

¼ cup maple syrup (60ml)

4 large egg yolks

Pinch of sea salt

1 tablespoon pure vanilla bean paste (15g)

1 shot of espresso

1. Whisk all of the ice cream ingredients together in a 4-quart pot.

2. Cook the mixture over medium heat and bring to just a simmer (about 10 to 15 minutes). While this is cooking you will need to whisk it from time to time to keep the mixture from sticking to the sides and bottom of the pan.

3. Since you're making a custard, you want it to be between 160 to 170 degrees Fahrenheit (71 to 77 degrees Celsius). To see if your custard is done, simply dip a spoon into the mixture and run your finger down the back of the spoon. If the line stays clean, your custard is done. If the line blurs again, you need a little more time to make the custard.

4. Remove from heat and let cool, at least 30 minutes. Pour into a refrigerator-safe container and cover with plastic wrap, making sure the plastic wrap is covering the top of the liquid (this keeps a skin from forming on top of your custard). Place this

into the refrigerator and chill for at least 6 hours. Overnight is best.

5. If the custard separates while cooling, simply stir it before pouring it into the ice cream maker.

6. Pour the chilled mixture into the ice cream maker and process according to the manufacturer's instructions.

7. Transfer to an airtight, freezer-safe container and freeze for 2 to 3 hours before serving.

8. Once the ice cream has frozen, remove it from the freezer and let it stand until it's scoopable. While you are waiting, you can make the espresso.

9. Scoop one or two balls of vanilla ice cream into a low glass or coffee cup. Top with the espresso.

~ HOT CHOCOLATE ~
WITH ICE CREAM

MAKES 2 SERVINGS

If you can have ice cream with coffee, why not have ice cream with hot chocolate? The two pair up to make an extremely delicious drink. That rich and thick hot chocolate with just a hint of chill from the vanilla ice cream is going to make your taste buds very happy.

PURE VANILLA ICE CREAM

MAKES 1 QUART

1. Whisk all of the ice cream ingredients together in a 4-quart pot.

2. Cook the mixture over medium heat and bring to just a simmer (about 10 to 15 minutes). While this is cooking you will need to whisk it from time to time to keep the mixture from sticking to the sides and bottom of the pan.

3. Since you're making a custard, you want it to be between 160 to 170 degrees Fahrenheit (71 to 77 degrees Celsius). To see if your custard is done, simply dip a spoon into the mixture and run your finger down the back of the spoon. If the line stays clean, your custard is done. If the line blurs again, you need a little more time to make the custard.

4. Remove from heat and let cool, at least 30 minutes. Pour into a refrigerator-safe

1 (13.5-ounce) can full-fat coconut milk (400ml)

1¾ cups full-fat coconut cream (420ml)

¼ cup maple syrup (60ml)

4 large egg yolks

Pinch of sea salt

1 tablespoon pure vanilla bean paste (15g)

container and cover with plastic wrap and make sure that plastic wrap is covering the top of the liquid (this keeps a skin from forming on top of your custard). Place this into the refrigerator and chill for at least 6 hours to chill thoroughly. Overnight is best.

5. If custard separates while cooling, simply stir it up before pouring it into the ice cream maker.

6. Pour the chilled mixture into an ice cream maker and process according to the manufacturer's instructions.

7. Transfer to an airtight, freezer-safe container and freeze for 2 to 3 hours before serving.

8. Once the ice cream has frozen, remove it from freezer and let it stand until it's scoopable. While you are waiting, you can make the hot chocolate.

9. Pour the coconut milk into a heavy-bottomed pan and add the unsweetened cocoa powder. Whisk to combine the cocoa powder and milk.

10. Heat the mixture over medium heat and add the cocoa butter. Continue whisking until the cocoa butter has melted.

11. Whisk in the maple syrup and vanilla, then remove from the heat.

12. Ladle the hot chocolate into 2 mugs and top with a scoop of vanilla ice cream.

FOR THE HOT CHOCOLATE

1 (13.5-ounce) can full-fat coconut milk (400ml)

½ cup unsweetened cocoa powder (42g)

2 tablespoons organic cocoa butter (30g)

¼ cup pure maple syrup (60ml)

1 teaspoon pure vanilla extract (5ml)

ICY FROZEN TREATS

~ STRAWBERRY ~
SORBET

MAKES 1 PINT

I think sorbet is one of the most perfect treats during the hot and steamy summer months. It's easy to make, doesn't require a lot of time, and is cool and refreshing. Because there are so few ingredients in sorbet, you can really taste the fruit that you use—make sure that you are using the best and freshest fruit you can find.

1. Remove the hulls from the strawberries and cut them into quarters.

2. Drop the strawberries, maple syrup, and lemon juice into the bowl of a food processor and pulse until everything is smooth. Brush down the sides to make sure all the pieces are puréed.

3. Chill the mixture for 3 to 4 hours.

4. Pour the mixture into the ice cream maker and process according to manufacturer's instructions, then freeze for 2 to 3 hours to firm up a bit more.

5. Alternately, you can pour the mixture into an 8 x 8 x 2-inch (20.32 x 20.32 x 5.08-centimeter) pan and freeze for 4 hours.

6. Break up the frozen mixture (it's easiest if you use a dinner knife for this) and drop the chunks into your food processor. Pulse it a few times just to break up the chunks and you'll see it get slushy (but not too slushy . . . you still want it thick). Then serve.

1 pound strawberries (454g)

⅓ cup maple syrup (120ml)

1 tablespoon freshly squeezed lemon juice (15ml)

~ LEMON ~
SORBET

MAKES 1 PINT

This crisp and tangy sorbet is a perfect summertime cooler, or a great palate cleanser when served during a big meal. You can serve it in little dishes or go all out and serve it in lemon cups for a very impressive presentation. This recipe is really simple (three ingredients) but brings so much flavor. I think you're going to love it.

1 cup water
½ cup raw honey (120ml)
1 cup freshly squeezed lemon juice (from 5–6 lemons)

1. Add the water and honey to a small, heavy-bottomed saucepan and heat until the honey is completely dissolved.

2. Remove the mixture from the heat and stir in the lemon juice.

3. Let the mixture cool, then pour it into a lidded container and chill in the refrigerator for at least 4 hours.

4. Stir, then pour the mixture into your ice cream maker and follow the manufacturer's instructions.

5. Scoop the sorbet into a freezer-safe, covered container and freeze for at least 2 hours before serving.

CUCUMBER PINEAPPLE SORBET

MAKES 1 QUART

Looking for something—anything—to help you cool down on that rocket-hot day? This Cucumber Pineapple Sorbet is just the thing. The cucumbers help to tone down the tartness of the pineapple and the sweetness in the pineapple ups the cooling flavor of the cucumbers. It's a very symbiotic relationship between these two ingredients. But one of the things that everyone says when they eat this is how refreshing it is.

1. Peel the cucumbers and cut them into 2-inch (5.08-centimeter) pieces.

2. Drop all of the ingredients into the blender and purée until everything is smooth (about 2 minutes).

3. Pour the ingredients into a refrigerator-safe container and cover. Chill for at least 4 hours. Chilling overnight is best.

4. Churn the sorbet in your ice cream maker according to the manufacturer's instructions.

5. Scoop the sorbet into a freezer-safe container and freeze for 2 to 3 hours to let it harden up a bit before serving.

1½ pounds hothouse or Persian cucumbers (680g)

¾ pounds pineapple chunks (340g)

¼ cup maple syrup (60ml)

2 tablespoons freshly squeezed lime juice (30ml)

1 teaspoon freshly squeezed lemon juice (5ml)

1 teaspoon pure vanilla extract (5ml)

PEACHES AND CREAM SORBET

MAKES 1 QUART

Okay, so sorbets traditionally don't have any dairy in them, but I really wanted to make a sorbet with a thin line of sweet cream through it (and, technically, this doesn't have dairy in it). Who says you have to stick to tradition? Eating this is almost like eating a bowl of peaches and cream. This is still a very light sorbet, as the cream is minimal and adds just a touch of flavor.

2 pounds peaches (907g)

6 tablespoons raw honey (90ml), divided

1 teaspoon freshly squeezed lemon juice (5ml)

Pinch of sea salt

½ cup coconut cream (120ml)

½ teaspoon pure vanilla extract

1. Pit and slice the peaches (peeling is optional).

2. Drop the peaches, 4 tablespoons honey, the lemon juice, and the salt into a blender or food processor and purée until everything is smooth.

3. Pour the mixture into a refrigerator-safe container, cover, and chill for at least 4 hours.

4. Pour the coconut cream, the remaining honey, and the vanilla into a small, heavy-bottomed pan. While this is heating, make sure to occasionally whisk to keep it from sticking and burning. Heat over medium high heat just until you see bubbles forming around the edges of the pan.

5. Pour this mixture into a refrigerator-safe container, cover, and chill for at least 4 hours.

6. Churn the peach sorbet mixture in your ice cream maker according to the manufacturer's instructions.

7. Scoop sorbet into a freezer-safe container and spread the cream mixture on top of the peach mixture. Freeze for 3 to 4 hours to let the sorbet harden up before serving.

~ ORANGE ~
SORBET

MAKES 1 PINT

Creamsicles and Orange Juliuses have been around forever, so why not let the orange have its own sorbet? This sorbet is light and sweet and when you use in-season oranges it's even sweeter (you may even need to use less honey). But the flavor in this sorbet is so unexpected it will make you smile with surprise and delight.

1. Add the honey, water, and orange zest to a medium, heavy-bottomed pan. Heat the mixture over medium-high heat, stir, and continue to cook until the honey has completely dissolved into the water. Remove the pan from heat and let cool.

2. Cut the peel and white pith from the oranges. Then cut the segments out of the oranges and drop them into the bowl of a food processor. As you finish cutting each orange, squeeze the remaining juice into the processor. Make sure you throw out any seeds.

3. Pulse the processor until everything is puréed and there are no pieces left.

4. Pour the orange purée into the honey mixture and stir to combine. Remove the pan from the heat and let cool.

½ cup raw honey (120ml)

½ cup water (125ml)

1 tablespoon orange zest (6g)

3 large oranges (about 1½ pounds) (680g)

5. Pour this mixture into a refrigerator-safe container, cover, and chill for at least 4 hours.

6. Churn the sorbet mixture in your ice cream maker according to the manufacturer's instructions.

7. Scoop the sorbet into a freezer-safe container, and freeze for 3 to 4 hours to let the sorbet harden up a bit before serving.

FROZEN PALEO

~ HONEY PEACH ~
SORBET

MAKES 1 QUART

Ever wonder what a Southern summer day tastes like? Well, you could inhale a mosquito or two while breathing in the hot humid air, or you could make a batch of this Honey Peach Sorbet instead. I prefer the sorbet, myself. The honey replaces the humidity with its lingering sweetness and peaches just scream summer day. These two things together are the perfect pairing.

2 pounds fresh or frozen peaches (910g)

1 teaspoon freshly squeezed lemon juice (5ml)

⅓–⅔ cup raw honey (80–160ml)

1½ teaspoons freshly grated ginger (3g)

Pinch of sea salt

1. Cut peaches into slices (don't peel them) and toss them into a food processor (minus the pits, of course). Add the lemon juice, honey, and ginger to the food processor as well, then purée until smooth.

2. Run the purée through a strainer to remove the skins.

3. Stir salt into the purée and give it a taste. Add more salt if you like.

4. Pour the mixture into a lidded container. Cover the container and chill for at least 4 hours (overnight is best) before churning in the ice cream maker according to the manufacturer's instructions.

5. Scoop the sorbet into a lidded container and freeze for 2 to 3 hours or until firm (adding more honey makes the freezing process take a bit longer).

6. Use less honey if your peaches are sweet and more honey if they aren't as sweet as you would like them to be.

~ ISLAND PARADISE ~
SORBET

MAKES 1 QUART

If you need a tropical paradise getaway, then this is the sorbet for you. The combination of mango, pineapple, banana, and coconut will bring to mind any number of tropical libations you may have had while digging your toes into the sand. Its smooth and creamy consistency will have you going back for more, more, and more.

1. Add all the ingredients to your blender and purée until everything is smooth.

2. You can serve this straight from the blender for a soft-serve consistency, or spoon it into your ice cream maker and let it go for about half the time the manufacturer suggests (because it's already pretty frozen).

3. Scoop it into a freezer-safe container and freeze for 2 to 3 hours to firm it up before serving.

½ cup raw honey (120ml)

¼ cup coconut cream (60ml)

2 tablespoons freshly squeezed lime juice (30ml)

1 (12-ounce) package frozen mango chunks (340g)

1 (16-ounce) package frozen pineapple chunks (455g)

1 medium ripe banana

~ CHERRY VANILLA ~
SORBET

MAKES 1 PINT

While cherries on their own are delicious, the shot of vanilla in this sorbet really helps brighten the flavor. Yes, I know that a sorbet that has cream in it is technically called a sherbet, but there's only enough cream in this to help richen the flavors, so I didn't call it a sherbet. However, you can call it whatever you like.

1 (16-ounce) package frozen sweet cherries (455 grams)

½ cup water (120ml)

¼ cup coconut cream (60ml)

1 tablespoon raw honey (15ml)

1 teaspoon freshly squeezed lemon juice (5ml)

1 teaspoon pure vanilla extract (5ml)

1. Add all the ingredients to your blender and purée until everything is smooth.

2. You can serve this straight from the blender for a soft-serve consistency, or spoon it into your ice cream maker and let it go for about half the time the manufacturer suggests (because it's already pretty frozen).

3. Scoop it into a freezer safe container and freeze for 2 to 3 hours to firm it up before serving.

~ MANGO ~
SORBET

MAKES 1 QUART

Like mangoes? Then you're going to love this fresh mango sorbet. It tastes exactly like the fruit, only creamier. You may notice that it's not quite as bright orange as typical mango sorbets go; that's because of the coconut palm sugar (which is pretty brown). But you do get a nice orange color out of it and the flavor is fantastically mango.

1. Add all of the ingredients to your blender and purée until everything is smooth.

2. Pour into a refrigerator-safe container, cover, and refrigerate for 6 hours or overnight to thoroughly chill.

3. Spoon the mixture into your ice cream maker and process according to the manufacturer's instructions.

4. Scoop the sorbet into a freezer-safe container and freeze for 2 to 3 hours to firm it up before serving.

2½–3 pounds mangoes, pitted, peeled, and chopped (about 3 mangoes) (1.13–1.36 kg)

¼ cup water (60ml)

¼ cup coconut palm sugar (50g)

3 tablespoons freshly squeezed lime juice (42ml)

~ LEMON-MINT ~
GRANITA

SERVES 4–6

Granitas are like sorbets' messier cousins. They aren't as refined (smooth and silky). Their ice crystals are jagged and lumpy and they can look a little strange sometimes. But you can't deny how refreshing they are, or their strong flavor. They're made very similarly to sorbets except you skip the machine part and rough them up every hour with a fork, so they're also easy to make. You may not think that lemon and mint go together, but they do. This tart granita is a perfect after-dinner treat. The mint is subtle in this one— you will taste it after the cold, refreshing ice crystals have melted on your tongue. I also like to serve this as a palate cleanser if I'm serving a big meal.

1 cup water (240ml)

¼ cup raw honey (60ml)

¼ cup loosely packed mint leaves (10g)

Lemon zest from 1 lemon

½ cup freshly squeezed lemon juice (from 3–4 lemons) (120ml)

1. Pour the water and honey into a small, heavy-bottomed saucepan, and heat over medium heat until honey has dissolved into the water. Remove the pan from the heat, stir in the mint leaves and zest and cover the pan. Let the mixture cool to room temperature.

2. Strain out the mint and lemon zest and add lemon juice to the syrup. Stir to make sure that everything is thoroughly combined.

3. Pour the mixture into an 8 x 8 x 2-inch (20.32 x 20.32 x 5.08-centimeter) pan and freeze it for 1 hour.

4. Bring the pan out of the freezer and use a fork to scrape whatever bits of it have frozen.

5. Return it to the freezer for another hour. Again use a fork to scrape whatever bits have frozen—you're creating ice crystals. You may need to do this I or 2 more times until you get the consistency you like. It really depends on how cold your freezer is.

6. Scrape again before serving.

~ KIWI LIME ~
GRANITA

SERVES 4–6

Don't you just love kiwi fruit? They're so cute and fuzzy. I especially like how the flavors of the fruit change as the fruit ripens. This granita can be made from kiwis at any stage of ripeness. I especially like it when the kiwi fruit are still a little bit hard, as they have more tang. Combine that with lime juice and you've got yourself a tart little treat with just a bit of sweetness. Like your granita a bit sweeter? Let those kiwi fruit ripen/soften a bit more. You'll have a delightfully sweet treat with the exotic flavor of kiwi.

1. Pour the water and honey into a small, heavy-bottomed saucepan, and heat over medium heat until honey has dissolved into the water. Remove the pan from the heat and let it cool to room temperature.

2. Add the kiwi fruit and lime juice to the bowl of your food processor and pulse until the mixture is puréed. You still want to see some of the little kiwi seeds though, so don't purée it too much.

3. Pour the mixture into an 8 x 8 x 2-inch (20.32 x 20.32 x 5.08-centimeter) pan and freeze it for 1 hour.

½ cup water (120ml)

7 tablespoons raw honey (105ml)*

6 kiwi fruits, peeled and cut into pieces

Freshly squeezed lime juice (from 3 limes)

---

* You may want to change the amount of honey you use depending on the sweetness of your kiwi fruit, so taste it after you blend everything together. If you need it to be more sweet, add the honey and give it another couple pulses in the food processor. But add the honey just a little at a time, because it is so sweet.

4. Bring the pan out of the freezer and use a fork to scrape whatever bits of it have frozen.

5. Return it to the freezer for another hour. Again use a fork to scrape whatever bits have frozen—you're creating ice crystals. You may need to do this 1 or 2 more times until you get the consistency you like. It really depends on how cold your freezer is.

6. Scrape again before serving.

~ BLOODY MARY ~
GRANITA

SERVES 4–6

This lovely little granita is a favorite of mine to serve at parties in the summer. We love a good Bloody Mary around our house, so we make up a big batch of this granita and serve it to our guests in shot glasses. It's a great way to get your party started. It's a little different for a granita, because there's no sugar in it, but it has a good swift kick of heat.

1½ cups tomato or vegetable juice (360ml)

3 tablespoons freshly squeezed lemon juice (45ml)

1 teaspoon horseradish (8g)

¼ teaspoon celery salt

⅛ teaspoon freshly ground black pepper

⅛ teaspoon tamari sauce

Few dashes of hot sauce

1. Add all the ingredients to a large bowl and stir to thoroughly combine.

2. Pour the mixture into an 8 x 8 x 2-inch (20.32 x 20.32 x 5.08-centimeter) pan and freeze it for 1 hour.

3. Bring the pan out of the freezer and use a fork to scrape whatever bits of it have frozen.

4. Return it to the freezer for another hour. Again use a fork to scrape whatever bits have frozen—you're creating ice crystals. You may need to do this 1 or 2 more times until you get the consistency you like. It really depends on how cold your freezer is.

5. Scrape again before serving.

~ WATERMELON ~
GRANITA

SERVES 4–6

This watermelon granita is a perfectly easy and delicious dessert for a summer get-together.

1. Add all the ingredients to a food processor or blender and purée until everything is smooth.

2. Pour the mixture into an 8 x 8 x 2-inch (20.32 x 20.32 x 5.08-centimeter) pan and freeze it for 1 hour.

3. Bring the pan out of the freezer and use a fork to scrape whatever bits of it have frozen.

4. Return it to the freezer for another hour. Again, use a fork to scrape whatever bits have frozen— you're creating watermelon ice crystals. You may need to do this 1 or 2 more times until you get the consistency you like. It really depends on how cold your freezer is.

5. Scrape again before serving.

4 cups cubed seedless watermelon (616g)

⅓ cup raw honey (120ml)

1 tablespoon freshly squeezed lime juice (15ml)

Zest from 1 lime

~ HIBISCUS ~
POPSICLES

MAKES 10 POPSICLES

These hibiscus popsicles are just what you need when you're looking for that little escape from the day-to-day. From their bright red color to their bright tropical flavor you'll swear you're lying in a hammock with a tropical breeze blowing through your hair. By buzzing up a bit of the hibiscus, mint, and ginger you get an extra hit of flavor and texture in these cool pops.

3 cups water (710ml)

½ cup raw honey (120ml)

1 cup dried hibiscus flowers (31g), divided

1-inch peeled and chopped ginger

¼ cup (loosely packed) mint leaves (10g)

2 tablespoons freshly squeezed lime juice (28g)

1. Bring the water to a boil in 4-quart pot. Remove the pot from the heat and add the honey and hibiscus flowers. Stir until the honey is completely dissolved. Let the flowers steep for one hour.

2. Strain the mixture (but save the flowers) into a high-speed blender.

3. Add ½ cup steeped flowers, chopped ginger, and mint leaves to the blender. Purée until smooth (about 1 minute), then stir in the lime juice.

4. Pour the liquid into popsicle molds and fill until about ¼ inch from the top (this will leave room for them to expand).

5. Freeze the popsicles for 6 to 8 hours. Insert popsicle sticks after 2 hours.

ORANGE CREAM POPSICLES

MAKES 12 POPSICLES

These easy-to-make popsicles will have you feeling like a kid again. They've got a great orange and cream flavor that tastes a lot like those old-timey favorites (the ones with the orange-wrapped cream center), but can be made in the comfort of your own kitchen.

1. Add all the ingredients to a high-speed blender and blend for one minute or until everything is well blended and smooth.

2. Pour the liquid into popsicle molds and freeze for 6 to 8 hours. Insert popsicle sticks after 2 hours.

1 (13.5-ounce) can full-fat coconut milk (400ml)
1 cup freshly squeezed orange juice (from 2–3 oranges) (237ml)
2 tablespoons raw honey (30ml)
1 tablespoon orange zest (15g)
½ teaspoon pure vanilla extract
Pinch of sea salt

BLUEBERRY POMEGRANATE POPSICLES

MAKES 6 POPSICLES

You know you should be eating more antioxidants, so why not make them delicious and fun at the same time? These Blueberry Pomegranate Popsicles are a pretty delivery system for those healthy antioxidants. To make them even better, angle those blueberries in the popsicle mold and you'll get blueberry and pomegranate in every bite.

1. In a small, heavy-bottomed saucepan heat the blueberries, 2 tablespoons honey, lemon juice, and cinnamon over medium heat. Cook the mixture and stir occasionally until it begins to thicken and get bubbly. Remove the pan from the heat and let it cool to room temperature.

2. Pour the blueberry mixture into a food processor or blender and buzz until mixture is smooth.

3. Now pour this mixture into your popsicle molds. Place the molds into the freezer. If you'd like, you can tip the molds on an angle, so that you'll get blueberry in every bite. Freeze for 2 hours.

2 cups frozen blueberries (240g)

3 tablespoons raw honey (45ml), divided

2 teaspoons freshly squeezed lemon juice (10ml)

⅛ teaspoon cinnamon

1 cup unsweetened pomegranate juice (240ml)

4. Add the pomegranate juice and 1 tablespoon honey to a heavy-bottomed saucepan and heat over medium heat. Cook until the honey has melted and combined with the juice. You'll need to stir this a little while the honey is melting. Remove the mixture from the heat and let it cool to room temperature.

5. Pull your popsicles from the freezer and carefully pour pomegranate juice into the molds. Place the popsicles back into the freezer and freeze for 2 hours. Remove the molds from the freezer and insert popsicle sticks. Put the molds back into the freezer and freeze overnight.

FROZEN PALEO

STRAWBERRY ~ & MANGO ~ COCONUT WATER POPSICLES

MAKES 5 POPSICLES OF EACH FLAVOR

When you just can't decide between strawberry or mango, make both! This simple popsicle layers in the creamy fruit with good-for-you coconut water. This layering not only makes for a pretty popsicle, but an interesting snack as well, as the different layers each have distinct textures.

1. For the mango popsicles, pour the coconut milk, mango chunks, and honey into a high-speed blender and blend until smooth and creamy. Pour into a bowl and set aside.

2. Clean out the blender and do the same with the coconut milk, strawberries, and honey.

3. Spoon the fruit purée into the bottom of the popsicle molds. You can do as little or as much as you like, but these will be layered with coconut water. I put about 1 inch of purée into the molds.

4. Put the popsicle molds into the freezer for one hour.

FOR THE MANGO POPSICLES

¾ cup + 2 tablespoons full-fat coconut milk (210ml)

1 cup frozen mango chunks (170g)

1 tablespoon raw honey (15ml)

Approximately 14 ounces (414ml) coconut water

FOR THE STRAWBERRY POPSICLES

¾ cup full-fat coconut milk (180ml)

1 cup frozen strawberries (330g)

1 tablespoon raw honey (15ml)

Coconut water

5. Remove the molds from the freezer and insert popsicle sticks, then layer in the coconut water. I added about 1½ inches of water to each mold. Place the molds back into the freezer for an hour. Continue this process until the molds are full.

6. Freeze overnight.

CREAMY CHOCOLATE POPSICLES

MAKES 6 POPSICLES

You loved those rich and creamy chocolate popsicles when you were a kid, so why not enjoy them as an adult? These dark, rich, and chocolaty popsicles will have you thinking you're a kid again, but with a more grown-up taste.

1. Whisk all of the ingredients together in a 4-quart pot.

2. Cook over medium heat and bring to just a simmer (about 10 to 15 minutes). While this is cooking you will need to whisk it to keep the mixture from sticking to the sides and bottom of the pan.

3. Since you're making a custard, you want it to be between 160 to 170 degrees Fahrenheit (71 to 77 degrees Celsius). To see if your custard is done, simply dip a spoon into the mixture and run your finger down the back of the spoon. If the line stays clean, your custard is done. If the line blurs again, you need a little more time to make the custard.

1 cup coconut cream (240ml)
½ cup full-fat coconut milk (120ml)
4 egg yolks
¼ cup maple syrup (60ml)
2 ounces baker's chocolate, melted* (57g)
⅓ cup unsweetened cocoa powder (28g)
1 teaspoon pure vanilla extract (5ml)
Pinch of sea salt

* To melt the baker's chocolate, chop it into small pieces and add the pieces to a small bowl. Heat in the microwave on high for 30-second intervals. Between each interval, remove the chocolate from the microwave and stir. Keep heating and stirring until the chocolate is completely melted.

4. Remove from heat and let cool, at least 30 minutes. Pour into a refrigerator-safe container and cover with plastic wrap, making sure the plastic wrap is covering the top of the liquid (this keeps a skin from forming on top of your custard). Place this into the refrigerator and chill for at least 6 hours to chill thoroughly. Overnight is best.

5. If the custard separates while cooling, simply stir it before pouring it into popsicle molds.

6. Pour the chilled mixture into popsicle molds and freeze for 2 hours. Insert popsicle sticks and freeze overnight.

CHOCOLATE-
~ DIPPED ~
PURE VANILLA
POPSICLES

MAKES 10 POPSICLES

When you just can't decide if you want vanilla or chocolate . . . why not have both? These creamy vanilla popsicles are coated in a thick, rich layer of chocolate, then topped with crushed, salted almonds. They're a creamy, crunchy, lightly sweet treat that will make you smile from ear to ear.

1. Whisk all of the ice cream ingredients together in a 4-quart pot.

2. Cook the mixture over medium heat and bring it to just a simmer (about 10 to 15 minutes). While this is cooking you will need to whisk it from time to time to keep the mixture from sticking to the sides and bottom of the pan.

3. Since you're making a custard, you want it to be between 160 to 170 degrees Fahrenheit (71 to 77 degrees Celsius). To see if your custard is done, simply dip a spoon into the mixture and run your finger down the back of the spoon. If the line stays clean, your custard is done. If the line blurs again, you need a little more time to make the custard.

FOR THE POPSICLES

1 (14-ounce) can full-fat coconut milk (414ml)

1¾ cups full-fat coconut cream (420ml)

¼ cup maple syrup (60ml)

4 large egg yolks

Pinch of sea salt

1 tablespoon pure vanilla bean paste (15g)

4. Remove from heat and let cool, at least 30 minutes. Pour into a refrigerator-safe container and cover with plastic wrap and make sure that plastic wrap is covering the top of the liquid (this keeps a skin from forming on top of your custard). Place this into the refrigerator and chill for at least 6 hours to chill thoroughly. Overnight is best.

5. If custard separates while cooling, simply stir it up before pouring it into the ice cream maker.

6. Pour the chilled mixture into the ice cream maker and process according to the manufacturer's instructions.

7. Spoon the mixture into popsicle molds. Freeze for 2 hours, then insert popsicle sticks. Continue freezing overnight.

8. Roughly chop the almonds and set aside.

9. In a small, deep bowl, mix the cocoa powder, coconut oil, and maple syrup until well blended.

10. Remove the popsicles from their molds and dip them into the chocolate one at a time.*

FOR THE TOPPING

½ cup roasted and salted almonds (164g)

¼ cup unsweetened cocoa powder (21g)

5 tablespoons coconut oil (75ml)

2 teaspoons maple syrup (10ml)

---

* Please note, there is not enough chocolate in this recipe to completely coat the popsicles. If you would like to completely coat each popsicle, simply double the topping recipe.

After dipping each one, roll it in the chopped nuts and then set on a plate or baking sheet.

11. Eat immediately or pop back into the freezer to freeze harder.

INDEX